Early Adventures in Algebra

Featuring Zero the Hero

GEMS® Teacher's Guide for Grades 1–2

by
Jaine Kopp

Skills

Computation (Addition, Subtraction) • Mental Math • Composing and Decomposing Numbers
Comparing the Magnitude of Numbers • Representing and Analyzing Mathematical Situations
Using Algebraic Symbols • Reflecting • Reasoning • Recording • Communicating • Graphing
Using Number Lines • Solving Equations • Writing Story Problems

Concepts

Zero • Zero as a Placeholder in Base 10 System • Place Value • Number Sense
Properties of Numbers and Operations • Identity Element of Addition
Commutative Property of Addition • Equality • Conventional Notation • Algebraic Notation
Greater Than, Less Than, Equal To

Themes

Systems and Interactions • Patterns of Ch

Mathematics Strands

Number • Functions and Algebra

Nature of Science and Mathematics

Cooperative Effort • Real-Life Applications

Time

Nine class sessions of 45–60 minutes;
two assessment sessions of 10–20 minutes

Great Explorations in Math and Science
Lawrence Hall of Science
University of California at Berkeley

Lawrence Hall of Science,
University of California,
Berkeley, CA 94720-5200

Director: Elizabeth K. Stage

Cover Design, Internal Design, and Illustrations: Lisa Klofkorn
Photography: Dan Krauss

Director: Jacqueline Barber
Associate Director: Kimi Hosoume
Associate Director: Lincoln Bergman
Mathematics Curriculum Specialist:
Jaine Kopp
GEMS Network Director:
Carolyn Willard
GEMS Workshop Coordinator:
Laura Tucker
Staff Development Specialists:
Lynn Barakos, Katharine Barrett, Kevin
Beals, Ellen Blinderman, Gigi Dornfest, John
Erickson, Stan Fukunaga, Karen Ostlund
Distribution Coordinator: Karen Milligan
Workshop Administrator: Terry Cort
Trial Test and Materials Manager:
Cheryl Webb
Financial Assistant: Vivian Kinkead
Distribution Representative:
Fred Khorshidi
Shipping Assistant: Justin Holley
Director of Marketing and Promotion:
Steven Dunphy
Principal Editor: Nicole Parizeau
Editor: Florence Stone
Principal Publications Coordinator:
Kay Fairwell
Art Director: Lisa Haderlie Baker
Senior Artists:
Carol Bevilacqua, Lisa Klofkorn

Staff Assistants: Marcelo Alba,
Kamand Keshavarz, Andrew Lee
Contributing Authors: Jacqueline Barber,
Katharine Barrett, Kevin Beals, Lincoln
Bergman, Susan Brady, Beverly Braxton,
Mary Connolly, Kevin Cuff, Linda De
Lucchi, Gigi Dornfest, Jean C. Echols, John
Erickson, David Glaser, Philip Gonsalves, Jan
M. Goodman, Alan Gould, Catherine
Halversen, Kimi Hosoume, Susan Jagoda,
Jaine Kopp, Linda Lipner, Larry Malone,
Rick MacPherson, Stephen Pompea, Nicole
Parizeau, Cary I. Sneider, Craig Strang,
Debra Sutter, Herbert Thier, Jennifer Meux
White, Carolyn Willard

Initial support for the origination and publication of the GEMS series was provided by the A.W. Mellon Foundation and the Carnegie Corporation of New York. Under a grant from the National Science Foundation, GEMS Leaders Workshops were held across the United States. GEMS has also received support from: the Employees Community Fund of Boeing California and the Boeing Corporation; the people at Chevron USA; the Crail-Johnson Foundation; the Hewlett Packard Company; the William K. Holt Foundation; Join Hands, the Health and Safety Educational Alliance; the McConnell Foundation; the McDonnell-Douglas Foundation and the McDonnell-Douglas Employee's Community Fund; the Microscopy Society of America (MSA); the NASA Office of Space Science Sun-Earth Connection Education Forum; the Shell Oil Company Foundation; and the University of California Office of the President. GEMS also gratefully acknowledges the early contribution of word-processing equipment from Apple Computer, Inc. This support does not imply responsibility for statements or views expressed in publications of the GEMS program. For further information on GEMS leadership opportunities, or to receive a publications catalog and the *GEMS Network News,* please contact GEMS. We also welcome letters to the *GEMS Network News.*

International Standard Book Number: 0-924886-77-3

Printed on recycled paper with soy-based inks.

Library of Congress Cataloging-in-Publication Data

Kopp, Jaine.
  Early adventures in algebra : featuring zero the hero / by Jaine Kopp.
    p. cm. -- (GEMS guides. Teacher's guides)
  ISBN 0-924886-77-3 (trade paper)
  1. Arithmetic--Study and teaching (Primary) 2. Zero (The number) I. Title. II. Series.
  QA135.6.K695 2004
  372.7--dc22

                                        2004006929

ACKNOWLEDGMENTS

Ever since I began teaching, Zero the Hero has been a beloved member of each of my classes. My thanks go to Zero, the amazing number that adds sparkle, wonder, power, and possibility to our base 10 system.

Zero the Hero became an important member of Lina Jane Prairie's second grade class at Edward M. Downer Elementary School during the initial trial test of the unit. Her students' enthusiastic participation in the *Early Adventures in Algebra* activities informed the development of the unit, as did Lina's insights and suggestions. Our heartfelt thanks and appreciation to Lina and her lively students, avid fans of Zero the Hero!

Thanks also goes to Kimi Hosoume, who served as my GEMS "buddy" during the first pilot test in Lina's class. Lincoln Bergman has a gift of verse and has crafted a special rhyming "performance piece" for this guide. Rhyme on, Lincoln!

The LUCIMATH programs, developed at the University of California Los Angeles under the direction of Dr. Shelley Krieger, made public valuable information on problem types researched at the University of Wisconsin–Madison by Dr. Thomas Carpenter, Dr. Elizabeth Fennema, and their colleagues. Their collective work on Cognitively Guided Instruction (CGI) provides a framework for understanding how children's mathematical thinking and problem-solving strategies develop. My thanks go to these and other mathematics professors for their commitment to supporting teacher education in mathematics content and pedagogy.

The students of Ana Laredo, Lina Prairie, Lisa Weaver, Michelle Edwards, and Pilar Marcos at Downer Elementary grace the photographs in this guide. Thanks to all of these young mathematicians and their dedicated teachers.

Many enthusiastic and supportive teachers across the country served as reviewers for *Early Adventures in Algebra* in its field test stages, and we deeply appreciate their valuable comments, classroom ideas, and samples of student work. Your insights and feedback helped us create a cohesive unit and develop Zero into a mathematical Super Hero! ■

CONTENTS

TIME FRAME

It's difficult to provide exact times for the length of each activity. Timing depends on many variables, such as your students' prior knowledge, their skills and abilities, your teaching style, "teachable moments" that arise, and many other factors. Based on classroom testing, the following are guidelines to help give you a sense of how long the activities may take.

Activity 1: Introducing Zero

Activity 2: Comparing Numbers

Activity 3: Moving on the Number Line

Activity 4: Solving Equations

Additional Assessment Activities

WHAT YOU NEED FOR THE WHOLE UNIT

The quantities listed below are based on a class size of 32 students. You may, of course, require different amounts for smaller or larger classes. This list gives you a concise "shopping list" for the entire unit. Please refer to the "What You Need" and "Getting Ready" sections for each individual activity, which contain more specific information about the materials needed for the class and for each student or student group.

Nonconsumables

- ☐ teacher read aloud: "Chapter 1: Zero Becomes Something" (page 19)
- ☐ teacher read aloud: "Chapter 2: Zero's Family" (page 40)
- ☐ teacher read aloud: "Chapter 3: Zero's Home" (page 59)
- ☐ teacher read aloud: "Chapter 4: Number Tricks" (page 76)
- ☐ teacher read aloud: "Chapter 5: One Last Trick Featuring Zero" (page 77)
- ☐ 32 small plastic frogs (or other animal or marker)
- ☐ 16 sets of base 10 materials★
- ☐ 16 bags or containers to hold the base 10 material
- ☐ 32 copies of the place value board (page 41 or 42)
- ☐ 32 standard dice
- ☐ 32 number lines
- ☐ *(optional)* counters
- ☐ *(optional)* 2 large standard dice (for teacher demonstration in Activity 2, Session 1)
- ☐ *(optional)* an overhead transparency of the **Into the Trash It Goes!** data sheet

★ Sources for base 10 materials can be found in the "Resources" section on page 116.

Consumables

- ☐ 1 copy of the **Letter to Families** (page 18)
- ☐ 32 mathematics journals
- ☐ 16 blank $\frac{3}{4}$ inch cubes (for making 0–3 dice)
- ☐ 96 self-adhesive, $\frac{1}{2}$-inch dots in two colors (48 of each color) to label cubes
- ☐ 16 copies of the **Zero, One, Two, Three: What Number Will It Be?** data sheet (page 20 or 21)
- ☐ 32 two-sided copies of the **Into the Trash It Goes!** data sheet (page 43 or 44)

❑ 32 two-sided copies of the **What's Missing?** mini-book template (pages 78–79)
❑ 32 two-sided copies of the **What's Missing? Find the Result** or **Find the Start** mini-book template (pages 80–81 or 82–83)

General Supplies

❑ several large sheets of chart paper, each about 24 in. x 36 in. (for class charts)
❑ markers
❑ masking tape
❑ transparent tape
❑ 1 permanent pen
❑ 32 scissors
❑ *(optional)* an overhead projector

INTRODUCTION

"**A**lgebra for first and second grade?" you might ask. YES is the resounding answer! Traditionally, algebra has not appeared in the mathematics curriculum until middle and high school. But there has been an important shift in mathematics education that advocates teaching elements of algebra—as well as other content areas in math—much earlier! Young children feel very "grown up" when they learn they're using algebra to solve problems.

Of course, in some respects the algebra young children learn does not look like the algebra that adults may recall from their high school days. This GEMS mathematics guide is designed to build a foundation in algebraic thinking and reasoning for students in the early primary grades that can be built upon throughout a student's mathematics education.

This GEMS guide features a special number—zero. Often thought of as "nothing" by students, they discover that zero really is quite something! Using the compelling context of "Zero the Hero," a mysterious and wonderful character, students learn the important role that zero serves in our base 10 number system. In computation, zero exhibits other unique properties. In addition, when zero is added to any number, the number remains unchanged (the identity element of addition). When zero is subtracted from a number, the number also remains unchanged. Later, students will learn that when any number is multiplied by zero, the result is zero.

Our word zero probably comes from the Latinized form zephirum *of the Arabic* sifr, *which in turn is a translation of the Hindu* sunya, *meaning "void" or "empty." The invention of the concept and symbol of "0" led to the development of the decimal (base 10) system.*

The activities in this guide provide learning experiences in which students use symbolic notation as they record equations derived from concrete situations. They solve for unknowns. Attention is given to the concept of equality—an integral part of algebra—as well as the meaning of inequality (greater than and less than). Throughout these activities, students represent and analyze mathematical situations using algebraic symbols.

The number standard is closely intertwined with algebra. In this unit, as students work with numbers appropriate to their skill levels, they practice computational and mental math skills, thereby improving facility with both numbers and operations.

As described in more detail on pages 4 and 5, this GEMS guide addresses the National Council of Teachers of Mathematics (NCTM)

Principles and Standards of School Mathematics for students in first and second grades. The activities build crucial scaffolding for more complex algebraic reasoning in later grades.

Overview of the Guide

Activity 1: Introducing Zero has two class sessions. In Session 1 students share their ideas and prior knowledge about zero. These ideas are recorded and referred to throughout the unit. In Session 2 students play a game with a special die to create numbers. Zero appears on three faces of the die, and the numbers 1, 2, and 3 are on the remaining three faces. Depending on their skill level, students create and record either a two- or three-digit number using the numbers they roll. After making five numbers, students identify their largest number. The activity introduces the concept of **zero as a placeholder in the base 10 system** and prepares students for work with zero in later activities.

Activity 2: Comparing Numbers also has two class sessions. Session 1 opens with the game Into the Trash It Goes! Students use the sum of two standard dice to determine the digits for numbers. As the title suggests, one of the numbers can be thrown "into the trash." After the numbers are created, students "decompose" them digit by digit into their place values. Students have an opportunity to see that **a number is equal to the sum of each of its digits' values.** In the second session, partners generate and compare numbers, using one standard die and the 0–3 die (from Activity 1). They calculate the sum of the dice to determine the value of the digits in numbers. These sums give students experience with zero as an addend. Then they build the numbers with base 10 blocks to compare magnitudes. Are the numbers equal? If not, which is greater? Students use the appropriate symbolic notation (=, >, or <) to record the relationship. This activity develops **algebraic thinking** with continued emphasis on deepening number sense and on **symbolic notation to represent equality and inequalities.** Again, zero plays a role as a placeholder.

Activity 3: Moving on the Number Line has three class sessions. Students use a small toy frog (or other animal) to move along a number line to represent the story of the frog's movements. In the first session, the answer to the final number story is always zero because that's the frog's home. The first movement the frog makes allows students to see zero's role as an addend. In the second session, the frog has moved to a new home, and the final answer to number stories is always the number 1. In the third session, students can start the frog on any number and end on a different number. They need to determine how the frog moved and what operation was used. As they play all three versions of the game, students see how the number line serves as a valuable mathematical tool. Students **represent and analyze mathematical situations using algebraic symbols.** They record equations that illustrate zero as the identity element of addition. Number facts are also reinforced, tying the Algebra standard together with the Number and Operations standard.

Activity 4: Solving Equations has two class sessions. Students generate equations with a missing number or "unknown" and solve for that unknown. Using dice to generate numbers for the equations, they record two parts of an equation in a mini-book. In Session 1, students determine the operation (addition or subtraction) needed to make the number sentence equivalent then solve for the missing number. They can use counting materials and/or a number line to provide support in calculating the answers. They also write a story that corresponds to and provides a context for the equation. In Session 2, other problem types are explored. This activity provides opportunities **to create equations** with the support of concrete materials. Students gain facility in **conventional notation.** As they record equations, zero can appear again as an addend, reinforcing its role as **the identity element of addition.** Different problem types are introduced and students learn that **an unknown can be situated in various locations** in equations.

Discourse and Class Content Knowledge

Throughout the unit, the teacher orchestrates the **classroom discourse** and encourages students to explain their thinking. To support learning, key concepts and algebraic symbols are recorded on a class chart. This chart serves as an important resource to provide access to content knowledge for all students. Student journal writing also reinforces the content. Like all GEMS guides, *Early Adventures in Algebra* provides you with clear step-by-step instructions. To further support classroom discourse, sample questions and **questioning strategies** are included in each activity to assist you in bringing out the mathematics. Encouraging students to express their thinking out loud and to explain their reasoning are critical aspects of teaching and learning mathematics content.

Children learn by thinking, discussing, and reflecting on what they have done.
—Dr. William Speer

Assessment

Throughout the unit, there are opportunities for ongoing assessment. This allows teachers to adjust their teaching so students are better able to grasp the concepts and skills. At the end of the unit, there are two **Additional Assessment Activities** in which students apply what they have learned throughout the unit. The information these assessments provide can also help guide subsequent instruction.

For greater focus on the algebra standard relating to "patterns, relations, and functions," we recommend activities in other GEMS units such as: the "Searches" activities in Group Solutions; "More Searches" and "Create a Creature" activities in Group Solutions, Too!; Activities 2–4 in Treasure Boxes; and "What Comes Next?" in Build It! Festival.

Early Adventures in Algebra and National Content Standards

Algebra Standards. The National Council of Teachers of Mathematics (NCTM) Algebra Standards for grades Prekindergarten–2 include: understanding patterns, relations, and functions; representing and analyzing mathematical situations and structures using algebraic symbols; using math models to represent and understand quantitative relationships; and analyzing change in various contexts. The activities in this unit most specifically address and will help your students develop these Algebra Standards:

- Represent and analyze mathematical situations and structures using algebraic symbols.

- Use mathematical models to represent and understand quantitative relationships.

Number and Operations Standards. Algebra is strongly connected to number sense in these early years, and this unit also addresses the following Number and Operations Standards:

- Understand numbers, ways of representing numbers, relationships among numbers, and number systems.

- Understand the meaning of operations and how they relate to one another.

- Compute fluently and make reasonable estimates.

Included under these broad headings are important skills related to place value, such as developing an understanding of the magnitude of numbers, and understanding the relationships among whole numbers by composing, decomposing, and grouping numbers.

The content in Early Adventures in Algebra *also addresses many state standards. Check your state guidelines to align the unit's content with your standards. Though many states have adopted the NCTM Standards, other states have modified them. In the California Mathematics Standards, for example, the activities in this unit specifically address the Grade 1 and Grade 2 Algebra and Functions Standard, and some Grade 3 standards. The unit also addresses the California Number Sense Standard for Grades 1 and 2.*

A Seed for Success

Algebra's real-world connections abound and student confidence in mathematics, success in higher education, and future career opportunities can all be deeply influenced by their encounters with algebra. Unfortunately, for a variety of reasons, algebra has attained a cultural reputation as complicated, difficult, and generally for "smart" students. This guide can plant a seed for young students' success in algebra by creating an interest in the subject, making it understandable, and laying a foundation to build on.

Though students are likely to progress at different rates and in different ways (which is to be expected), *all* students should be able to grasp the concepts in this guide, and to do so with enthusiasm and confidence instead of the anxiety often associated with algebra. Students are also highly likely to develop a new appreciation for an important number that holds these activities together—none other than "***Zero the Hero***"!

Special Feature: Math Stories!

Interspersed in this guide are five short read-aloud stories featuring Zero the Hero, the Queen of Numbers, and other numbers. As you read them aloud, you may want to write any unusual words on the board. In some cases, it may be helpful to go back over several sentences and write the calculation the sentences describe on the board. We hope the stories are enjoyable and useful.

There is also a "performance piece" hip-hop rhyme by Zero the Hero. You may want to use some or all of it as a poetic math extension for your class! ■

© 1999 Randy Glasbergen.

"I'm paid $4,000,000 a year. You're paid $40,000. The only difference is a few zeros. Everyone knows that zero equals nothing. So what's the problem?"

Zero is nothing, but nothing bad. — First Grade Student (Ruth's class)

Overview

Zero is arguably the most important number in our base 10 system! Without zero, we would not have a base system because there would be no placeholder to allow us to generate large numbers. Take the number 100 for example. If zero was not written in to represent "zero tens" and "zero ones" in this number, it would simply be 1. Zero is a quantifier and names a group without any objects in it. Sparking students' interest and curiosity in the number zero will help deepen their conceptual understanding of its multifaceted role in mathematics.

The unit opens with students sharing their ideas and knowledge about the number zero. These ideas are recorded on a class chart to be referred to throughout the unit. In some classes, students may have lots of ideas about zero, while in other classes, students may have limited knowledge. This brainstorming serves as a pre-assessment, and identifies prior knowledge and possible misconceptions.

In Session 1, just bringing the idea of zero to the fore is what is most important. It's also important to have your students generate questions about zero. As the unit evolves, zero takes on a persona and becomes known as "*Zero the Hero.*"

In Session 2, students are introduced to a game called Zero, One, Two, Three: What Number Will It Be? Using a special die with the numbers 0, 1, 2, and 3, students roll and record either a two- or three-digit number. Zero the Hero appears on three faces of the die, and the numbers 1, 2, and 3 appear one time each on the remaining three faces. Zero's prominence on the die provides an opportunity for students to record zeros in the place values of the numbers they create.

The game is a way to discuss zero's role and importance as a placeholder in the base 10 system. Whether or not the magnitude of a number is affected depends on the location of zero in that number. For example, 01 is simply the number 1—the zero is a placeholder in the ten's place and represents 0 tens in the number. In that case, the magnitude of the number is not affected by the placement of the zero. On the other hand, the number 10 represents one ten and zero ones. The zero in the one's place is significant, because without it the number would only be 1. The game helps spur student interest in zero, and there will be more about zero throughout the unit. After doing these activities, we might play on and modify the first grade student's initial comment above to say instead—*"Zero is something, and something good!"*

Session 1:
What We Know and Wonder about Zero

■ What You Need

For the class:
- ❑ several pieces of chart paper
- ❑ markers
- ❑ masking tape

For each student:
- ❑ 1 copy of the **Letter to Families** (page 18)

■ Getting Ready

1. Prepare two charts on 24 inch x 36 inch pieces of paper with the following headings:

   • Our Ideas about Zero

   • What We Wonder about Zero

   Have blank chart paper available in case your students come up with lots of ideas about zero.

2. Read the **Letter to Families** on page 18. Duplicate it or make your own version to send home with your students.

3. Before you present the session, gather markers, masking tape, the two pre-made charts, and extra chart paper.

 ### ■ Zero the Hero

1. Write the word "zero" on the board. Have students read the word. Have students talk to a person sitting close to them, sharing what they know about zero.

2. As they talk, post the chart, "Our Ideas about Zero." After a few minutes regain the attention of the class and ask them to share their ideas.

3. As students share, record their ideas. Encourage each student to **explain** the statement she or he suggests. Check with the class to see if they agree with each statement made about zero.

4. Continue to call on students and discuss what each student says. Even when there is disagreement, it's important to record the idea. Those that are controversial can be marked with a question mark or another symbol.

5. When your students have finished expressing their ideas, ask them what they wonder about zero and want to find out more about.

6. Post the second chart, "What We Wonder about Zero," and record their responses.

7. Let the class know this is the start of a new unit in math. It features zero and some interesting ways to think about numbers.

8. As a homework assignment, ask students to talk to their families about zero. Have them find out what their families know about zero to share with the class.

9. Distribute the **Letters to Families** for students to take home.

> *In one class of second graders, the teacher was surprised at how much knowledge the students had. For example, they knew that if zero was added to any number, the sum was that same number. Also, they knew that if you added zeros "behind" (to the right of) a (whole) number, the number would grow in magnitude. (Note: the qualifier "whole" in parentheses is for accuracy, because, in later years, when students encounter decimals, they will see that adding a zero to the end (right side) of a decimal will **NOT** increase its value—in that case the value of the number will remain the same—.5 and .50 are equivalent.)*

Session 2: Zero, One, Two, Three: What Number Will It Be?

■ What You Need

For the class:
- ❏ several pieces of chart paper
- ❏ markers
- ❏ 1 permanent pen
- ❏ teacher read aloud: "Chapter 1: Zero Becomes Something" (page 19)
- ❏ masking tape

For each pair of students:
- ❏ 1 blank $\frac{3}{4}$ inch cube for die
- ❏ 6 self-adhesive, $\frac{1}{2}$-inch dots in two colors (three dots of each color) for labeling the cube

❑ 1 copy of the **Zero, One, Two, Three: What Number Will It Be?** data sheet (for 1s and 10s, page 20; for 1s, 10s, and 100s, page 21)

For each student:
❑ mathematics journal

■ Getting Ready

1. To make the dice for the game:

Note: The dice made for this session are used again in Activity 2, Session 2.

a. Gather enough blank wooden or plastic cubes so there will be one for each pair of students.

b. Place a single dot of one color (blue) on three faces of each cube and a single dot of another color (yellow) on the remaining three faces. (Of course you may substitute colors, depending on the dots you may have on hand, as long as there are three dots each of two colors.)

c. Write the number 0 on all three blue dots with a permanent pen.

d. For the three yellow dots, write the number 1 on one, the number 2 on another, and the number 3 on the third. The dice should now have three faces with the number 0 on one color (blue), and on the other color (yellow) one face with the number 1, one face with the number 2, and one face with the number 3.

2. Decide which version of the **Zero, One, Two, Three: What Number Will It Be?** data sheet you will use with your class. Depending on their skills and abilities, select the one with two-digit numbers from page 20 or the one with three-digit numbers from page 21.

3. Make a two-sided sheet for each pair of students by copying the data sheet you selected on both sides of the paper.

4. Make or purchase a mathematics journal for each student. We have found that a special journal for the topic of "Algebra" adds to the excitement and enthusiasm of the unit. However, if your students already have a journal, they can continue using that one. **They will use the journal throughout the unit.**

5. On a piece of chart paper, write "What We Learned." This chart will be used to record what students learn in this activity and will also be added to throughout the unit.

6. Label another piece of chart paper with the heading, "Further Investigations," to record ideas about zero that are in question and need further information to prove or disprove.

7. Read over the story "Chapter 1: Zero Becomes Something" (page 19) to familiarize yourself with it before reading it out loud near the end of the session.

8. Just before you teach students the game, have dice and data sheets handy to distribute to partners. Gather the markers and masking tape, and have the two pre-made charts ready to post at the end of the game.

 ## ■ Introducing the Game

1. Review students' ideas about zero and ask about their families' ideas.

2. Help them report by asking questions, such as, "Did your families agree with any of our ideas about zero?" "If so, what idea(s)?" Ask for examples.

3. As students respond with new information, modify the "Our Ideas about Zero" or "What We Wonder about Zero" charts created in Session 1 as appropriate.

4. Tell students you have a game for them to play. Show them the **Zero, One, Two, Three: What Number Will It Be?** data sheet. Have students read the title.

5. Tell students the game is played with a special die with numbers on it. The numbers on the faces of the die are 0 (also known as Zero the Hero), as well as 1, 2, and 3. **Do not emphasize that zero is on three faces.**

6. Tell students this game is played with a partner and players take turns rolling the die. Each player will use the numbers rolled to make either a two- or three-digit number (depending on the data sheet you've selected for your class).

7. Refer again to the data sheet. Review the names of the place values for the numbers students will make (tens and ones for two-digit numbers; hundreds, tens, and ones for three-digit numbers).

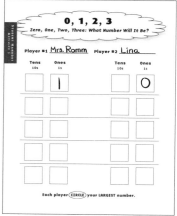

8. Demonstrate how to play the game with a student partner:

a. Write your name on the data sheet next to Player #1. Have your partner write her name next to Player #2.

b. Point out the digit boxes where you'll record the numbers you roll. Have students tell you the magnitude of the numbers they'll record (ones, tens, hundreds).

c. Roll the die first. Record your number in a digit box for the first number located under your name as Player #1. (You can place the number you roll in any of the boxes for the first turn—either the ones or tens box, if playing with two digits; or the ones, tens, or hundreds box, if playing with three digits.)

d. Next, Player #2 rolls the die and records the number in one of the digit boxes on her side of the data sheet below her name.

e. Players continue to roll the die and generate numbers for all the digits for **their first numbers.**

f. Next, they continue to roll the die and record the digits for the second number.

g. Players continue by filling in the third, fourth, and fifth numbers.

h. When all five numbers have been filled in, each player circles her largest two- (or three-) digit number.

■ Playing the Game

1. After students understand how the game is played, distribute a data sheet and a die to each pair of students. Let the games begin!

2. Circulate as the students play and assist as necessary. Have those students who finish before others turn over their data sheets and play again.

3. When everyone has filled in all the digits for five numbers and identified their highest number, focus attention for a group discussion.

4. Ask questions to help students analyze how they used the zero in creating numbers, such as:

• How many used a zero as a digit in the ones place? tens place? hundreds place?

- If you rolled two zeros and one number 3 what is the largest number you can make? the smallest number?

- What is the largest number you could make using the numbers on the die? What is the smallest number?

- How can you use a zero to make a number larger? Have students give examples as they explain.

- How can you use a zero to make a number smaller? Have students give examples as they explain.

- Why do you think zero is an important number?

5. At the end of the discussion, ask students what they learned about zero. Have them first talk to their game partners about this, before they discuss it as a class.

6. As they are talking with each other, post the two new charts, "What We Learned" and "Further Investigations."

7. Now have students express and explain what they learned in a class discussion. Record explanations that are accurate. If they give ideas that are not accurate *or* if you are unsure about their accuracy, record those ideas on the "Further Investigations" chart. Say that these are interesting ideas that need more research.

8. Pass out a journal to each student. Ask them to write their names on the journals and label them as "mathematics journal." Explain that these will be their special journals just for math, and they'll use them to write down important math information.

9. Provide time for students to record what they learned about zero in their journals. They can take ideas from the class chart or write their own thoughts about why zero is important. Mention the name "Zero the Hero" and ask, "What does hero mean?"

10. Collect students' journals at the end of the activity to assess what they have recorded. This can provide an informal assessment of their work and help you decide where to begin the next activity.

11. Read out loud the story on page 19 entitled "Chapter 1: Zero Becomes Something." You may want to write key words, big ideas, or numbers on the board as you read. Actively involve the students in the story. Encourage comments and discussion. Tell students that there will be more "Zero the Hero" stories.

*As they play, some students may notice that they roll zero more frequently than any other number. This may spark a discussion about the die, with students saying it is not a "fair" die. Since zero occurs three times out of a possible six, there is a 50% or 1 in 2 chance of rolling a zero. In contrast, each of the other numbers occurs only one time, so there is a 16.6% or 1 in 6 chance of rolling a 1, 2, or 3. The Graphing Zero Going Further on page 16 can help students **understand** these proportions **concretely,** without explaining the idea of probability more abstractly.*

■ Going Further

1. Graphing Zero

a. Since zero occurs so frequently on the die, have students investigate how many total times zero was rolled.

b. Have them count the total number of zeros they rolled and recorded on their data sheets (one side of the data sheet only).

c. Distribute a Post-it® Note to each student. Ask them to record the number of times they rolled zeros on it.

d. Make and post a chart with the title, "Number of Times We Rolled Zero the Hero" showing the range of the number of times a zero could be rolled.

e. If your students made two-digit numbers, the number of times possible for rolling a zero ranges from 0 to 10. If they made three-digit numbers, the number of times possible for rolling a zero ranges from 0 to 15.

f. Have students place their Post-it Notes on the chart above the number that represents how many times they rolled a zero.

g. After all the data is posted, ask for their observations about the graph. Encourage students to articulate facts about the graph first. For example, "Seven people rolled zero three times." or "Everyone rolled at least one zero." Pose questions to help focus the discussion as necessary.

h. After the facts about the graphs are shared, ask students what the graph tells them or leads them to think. These are inferences. For example, a student could say, "When you play the entire game with this die, you will always roll a zero."

i. The finale is to determine how many zeros were rolled as a grand total by the entire class. Have students work in partners to determine the number. As they share results, be sure to have them explain how they arrived at their totals.

Number of Times We Rolled
ZERO the HERO

| 0 | 1 | 2 | 3 | 4 | 5 | 6 | 7 | 8 | 9 | 10 |

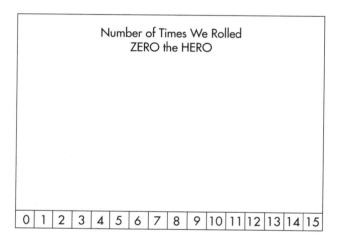

Number of Times We Rolled
ZERO the HERO

| 0 | 1 | 2 | 3 | 4 | 5 | 6 | 7 | 8 | 9 | 10 | 11 | 12 | 13 | 14 | 15 |

2. "The Number One" (or Two or Three) Graph

Have students follow the same steps for the zero graph to create a graph for the number 1 (or 2 or 3). Label the chart appropriately, such as: "Number of Times We Rolled the Number One."

3. Comparison of Graphs

Have students compare the graph, "Number of Times We Rolled Zero the Hero," with the graph, "Number of Times We Rolled the Number One." This could lead to an interesting discussion about the probability of rolling a zero versus a one. The die is "unfair" in the sense that there are three chances out of six to roll a zero, and one chance out of six to roll a one. It is likely the data will show that zero had an advantage by occurring more times on the die.

4. Spinners as a Random Number Generator

Instead of using the die to generate numbers in the game, use a spinner. Divide a spinner into six **equal** parts. Label three parts with zeros. Label the other three parts with the numbers 4, 5, and 6. Alternatively, divide a spinner into eight **equal** parts. Label four parts with zero and the others with the numbers 6, 7, 8, and 9. These spinners will provide a chance to create larger numbers.

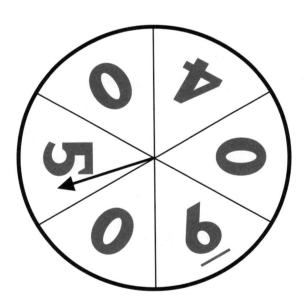 

LETTER TO FAMILIES

Dear Families,

Today we started a new mathematics unit focused on algebraic thinking. Although algebra has been considered a subject for upper grades, the work we are doing now builds a solid foundation for later years. Research shows that introducing very young students to algebraic ideas sets the stage for later success!

We began with a discussion about the number zero. The students shared their ideas about zero and raised questions they have about zero. Tonight, your child will ask you what you know about zero. After you share an idea or two, ask them what they know or wonder about zero. Tomorrow the students will share the ideas from their families, and we will add any new information to our class charts, "*Our Ideas about Zero*" and "*What We Wonder about Zero.*"

Over the next few weeks, our math work will focus on the important role of zero in our base 10 number system as well as some of the special properties of zero. For example, they will learn that any number plus zero is equal to that number ($0 + n = n$ and $n + 0 = n$), known formally as the Identity Property of Addition.

We will also compare numbers and use number lines for addition and subtraction problems. The students will solve problems with an "unknown" and use the notation for equations and inequalities. Computational strategies will also be introduced.

Be sure to ask your child what we are doing in class and please come into our classroom to read our charts and check the "*What We Learned*" chart for additional updates.

Thank you for your support of our mathematics program!

Chapter 1: Zero Becomes Something

Once upon a time in the Land of Numbers, there were only the digits, 0, 1, 2, 3, 4, 5, 6, 7, 8, and 9.

In that land, the numbers did not always treat one another very well. The larger numbers liked to tease the smaller numbers.

If a 6 met a 2, the 6 would say, "I'm more than you!"

Now you can just imagine how Zero was treated. Zero was teased by the other numbers more than any other. They said Zero was a nothing!

For instance, one morning Zero was walking along and met the number 4. As soon as 4 saw Zero, 4 started teasing Zero. "Ha! Ha! I'm more than you!"

Zero felt bad and walked away. Four was right, Zero thought. Four is more than Zero.

Zero kept walking and along came the number 7. Seven did the same thing to Zero that 4 did. Seven said, "Ha! Ha! I'm more than you are!" Then 7 added, "You're a nothing!"

Then, Zero saw 8 and for a minute, Zero felt happy. Eight looks so much like Zero…it seemed that 8 was a Zero with a belt on.

Zero asked 8, "Where did you get that cool belt?" Eight did not understand Zero. However, 8 was very even-tempered and more kind than the other numbers, and 8 just said, "Have a great day, Zero!"

Zero saw number 9 sitting alone on a bench. Nine looked very worried. Zero asked 9 if he was OK. Nine said he knew all the numbers that came before him, but he did not know what came after. Nine said he knew 0, 1, 2, 3, 4, 5, 6, 7, and 8.

He asked Zero if she knew what came next. Zero didn't know either.

Zero suggested that they go to the Queen of Numbers.

When they got there, the Queen had a great idea. She called for the number 1. The Queen said that there was an important job to be done and only Zero could do it. Then she turned to Zero and asked for help.

The Queen asked, "Will you walk next to the number 1, so that we can make the next largest number—the number 10?"

Zero was honored. The other numbers gathered around and they could not believe their eyes. Zero had become something! Zero made the 1 into a 10 and 10 was more than 9, 8, 7, 6, 5, 4, 3, 2, and 1.

From that day on, the other numbers had a lot of respect for Zero.

Zero also paired up with 2 and together they created the number 20. You can imagine all the other numbers wanted Zero as a partner, and so the numbers 30, 40, 50, 60, 70, 80, and 90 came into being.

All because of Zero. Now that really is something!

0, 1, 2, 3

Zero, One, Two, Three: What Number Will It Be?

Player #1 _____   Player #2 _____

Tens	Ones		Tens	Ones
10s	1s		10s	1s

Each player CIRCLE your LARGEST number.

0, 1, 2, 3

Zero, One, Two, Three: What Number Will It Be?

Player #1 _____   **Player #2** _____

Hundreds 100s	Tens 10s	Ones 1s	Hundreds 100s	Tens 10s	Ones 1s
☐	☐	☐	☐	☐	☐
☐	☐	☐	☐	☐	☐
☐	☐	☐	☐	☐	☐
☐	☐	☐	☐	☐	☐
☐	☐	☐	☐	☐	☐

Each player CIRCLE your LARGEST number.

Overview

The first session of this activity presents a new game called Into the Trash It Goes! Students roll two standard dice and calculate the sum of the numbers on the dice. They use that sum to fill in a digit's place on their data sheets. Since the possible sums of two dice include the numbers 10, 11, and 12, and students can only record a one-digit number in each box, the numbers 10, 11, and 12 are recorded as a zero. When Zero the Hero is one of the digits in the number, it serves as a placeholder and can make a number larger or smaller.

At first, partners aim for the largest number possible. As they roll and generate numbers, they strategize the best placement for each number rolled. After the players fill in the digits' places for their numbers, students break apart or "decompose" their numbers to analyze the place value of each digit.

After they are familiar with and have discussed the game and recorded ideas in their journals, they should also play the game with the aim of making the *smallest* number possible. For further practice, they can then decide with their partners whether to play for the highest or lowest possible numbers.

In Session 2 partners roll a standard die and the 0 to 3 die (from Activity 1) and calculate the sum. Then they record their numbers in digits' places—from the one's place to the ten's place or hundred's place—in their journals. After each partner has recorded a number, they compare the magnitudes of their numbers to determine which number is greater—or if the numbers are equal. Students use the appropriate symbol (> , < , or =) to record the relationship between the numbers.

Once again, Zero the Hero plays a key role in creating numbers. In this activity, **zero's importance in the base 10 system is reinforced** as students **compose and decompose numbers.** This activity also provides students with practice in **analyzing and comparing the magnitude of numbers** and **using notation to represent equality and inequalities.** Zero's identity property is introduced informally through creating sums.

For example, using the number 352, the number 3 represents three 100s and has a value of 300—not 3. Similarly, the 5 in the number represents five 10s and has a value of 50. In decomposing the number in this way, students see that the number 352 is equal to the sum of its place value parts, 300 + 50 + 2 = 352. The place value of the digits impacts the magnitude of the number.

Students are likely to roll 0 as an addend when calculating sums. This provides an opportunity to see zero as the identity element of addition.

Session 1: Into the Trash It Goes!

■ What You Need

For the class:

❑ "What We Learned" chart from Activity 1, Session 2
❑ "Further Investigations" chart from Activity 1, Session 2
❑ markers
❑ teacher read aloud: "Chapter 2: Zero's Family" (page 40)
❑ *(optional)* 2 large dice
❑ *(optional)* an overhead transparency of the **Into the Trash It Goes!** data sheet
❑ *(optional)* an overhead projector

For each pair of students:

❑ 1 set of base 10 materials★ (wooden or plastic) in the following approximate denominations:

    ____ 20 ones (small cubes, also known as units)
    ____ 20 tens (rods, also known as longs)
    ____ 18 hundreds (flats) *if* your students are working with numbers through the hundred's place

❑ 1 bag or container to hold the base 10 material
❑ 2 copies of the place value board (for two-digit numbers, page 41; for three-digit numbers, page 42)
❑ 2 standard dice
❑ 2 copies of the **Into the Trash It Goes!** data sheet (for two-digit numbers, page 43; for three-digit numbers, page 44)

For each student:

❑ mathematics journal

★Sources for base 10 materials can be found in the "Resources" section on page 116.

If you do not have these blocks, check with other teachers at your school to borrow them for a few days. They are also used in the next session.

■ Getting Ready

1. Depending upon your students' skills and abilities, select either the **Into the Trash It Goes!** data sheet with two-digit numbers (on page 43) or the sheet with three-digit numbers (on page 44). If you've decided to use the data sheet on the overhead, make a transparency of it.

2. Copy the data sheet you've selected on to both sides of a sheet of paper. Make one per student (pairs of students will have two copies to enable them to play several games) as well as several extra sheets.

3. Make two copies of the place value board (page 41 or 42, depending on which data sheet you've selected) for each pair of students.

4. For each student pair, gather the base 10 material.

5. Have the bags of base 10 material, dice, place value boards, and data sheets ready to distribute **after** modeling how to play the game with the class.

6. Read over the story "Chapter 2: Zero's Family" (page 40) to familiarize yourself with it before reading it out loud to the class.

7. Have markers available to add to the "What We Learned" chart (which was posted at the end of Activity 1, Session 2).

■ Sum of Two Standard Dice

1. Review the "What We Learned" chart. Check that everyone understands and agrees with what has been recorded.

2. Tell students you have a new game for them to play. Let them know that in this game they will make numbers by rolling standard dice.

3. Ask students what they know about standard dice. You may want to prompt them with some of the following questions:

   • What games have they played with dice?

   • What geometric shape is a die?

   • How many sides or faces does it have?

   • Is there a 0 on a standard die?

   • Do dice always have dots on the faces?

4. Show them a pair of standard dice. (Use the large dice if you have them.) Have students talk to a partner about what numbers can be made with two standard dice.

5. Ask the students to share their ideas about the numbers, and write on the board the possible sums (2 through 12) and some of the ways you can get those numbers. Make sure they understand that, when using the sum of two standard dice, the number 1 cannot be obtained.

6. Remind students they'll use these dice to play a game called Into the Trash It Goes! In this game, they are going to roll the dice to create numbers that will make a two- (or three-) digit number (depending on which data sheet you've chosen).

■ Introducing the Game

If you've made a transparency, you can display the data sheet on the overhead projector.

To help students remember that only one numeral can be written for each digit in a number, you could make an analogy to baseball. Ask them if they know how many runners can be safe on a single base at the same time. Some are likely to know that only one runner can occupy a base at a time. In a similar way, only one numeral can occupy a digit's place at any one time.

1. Show students the data sheet for the game. Have students identify the place values of the number they will build. [Tens, ones **OR** hundreds, tens, ones.]

2. Tell them that they will use the *sum* of the dice to fill in the digits on their sheets. Ask if any of the sums rolled will be difficult to record. [10, 11, and 12, because they have more than one digit.]

3. Let students know that in this game, when the sum of the roll is a 10, 11, or 12, they will record a 0. This means they can record the numbers 0, 2, 3, 4, 5, 6, 7, 8, or 9 on their sheets. The only number that **cannot** be recorded is a 1.

4. Tell students that for now the object of the game is to make the **highest** number possible, using the sums they roll. Later they will play the same game, but with the object of making the lowest number possible.

5. Point out the "trash can" on the sheet. Explain that one of the sums they roll can be "thrown" into the trash. That's why the game is called Into the Trash It Goes!

6. With a student partner, demonstrate how to play the game and record on the data sheet as follows:

a. Write your name next to Player #1. Have your partner write her name next to Player #2.

b. Circle the word **HIGHEST** to identify the magnitude of number you are each trying to make.

c. Review the place values of the numbers you will make. Point out the boxes to record numbers in the digit's places OR in the trash can. The trash can is used for the *one* number **you do not want to record** as one of the digits in your number. **Once a number is recorded in a digit's place or in the trash, it cannot be changed. And once there is a number in the trash can, it is "full" and can no longer be used.**

d. Player #1 rolls the dice first and calculates the sum.
   If the sum is 2-9, record that number in one of the boxes *or* in the trash can.
   If the sum is 10, 11, or 12, record a 0 in one of the boxes *or* in the trash can.

e. Next player #2 rolls the dice and records a number in one of the boxes or in the trash can, using the same rules as Player #1.

f. Players take turns rolling the dice and recording numbers in the digits' places and the trash can until all are filled.

For example, in a demonstration game, the results after four rolls per player were:

Player #1: Ms. Lakey   Player #2: Chazz

        Trash   Trash
637   4   497   5

7. Next, demonstrate how players will **build their numbers using base 10 materials.** In this example, the numbers would be built on place value boards as shown.

8. Below the numbers on the data sheet, **break down (or decompose) the numbers into their place value parts,** so that each number is the sum of each of its digit's values. In this case:

Player #1: Ms. Lakey   Player #2: Chazz

       Trash   Trash
637   4   497   5

  600   400
   30   90
+ 7   + 7
―――   ―――
637   497

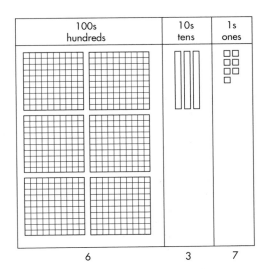

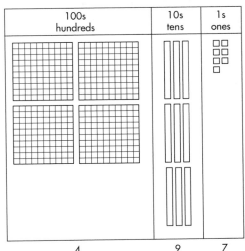

Note: The decomposition allows students to see each number in its expanded form. Connect the written numbers to the representation with base 10 material.

■ Partners Play the Game

In later games, students will be given the choice of whether to aim for the highest or the lowest number.

1. As needed, review how to play the game and respond to any questions students may have about it. Say that for the first two games, everyone should try to make the highest number possible. Remind them to circle the word HIGHEST at the top of the data sheet.

2. Distribute dice, place value boards, data sheets, and base ten material to pairs of students. As students play the game, circulate to assess how well they are doing. Assist as necessary.

3. When most pairs have played two games, focus the class for a discussion. Pose questions, such as:

  • What is the highest possible number that can be made? [99 or 999.]

  • Did anyone make a number close to 99/999 or in the 90s/900s?

4. Call on several students and record their numbers on the board. Determine the largest. Order the numbers from highest to lowest.

5. Ask questions to focus thinking and discussion, such as:

  • Did anyone get the sum of 10, 11, or 12 and have to record a zero?

  • If the trash was already filled, what digit's place did you put the zero in? Why?

  • Where would you place a zero to keep the number as *large* as possible? [One's place.]

  • Where would you place a zero to make the number as *small* as possible? [Hundred's place.]

  • What strategies did you use to create the largest number?

6. Record their strategies for making the largest number possible.

7. If necessary, pass out more data sheets then provide time for partners to play the game again, only this time the object is to make the lowest number possible. Remind them to circle the word LOWEST on the data sheet.

8. When students have completed all of their data sheets, encourage them to continue playing and to record their numbers in their journals.

9. As students finish, ask if anything new can be added to the "What We Learned" chart. Record any new insights your students have. The list may include, for example:

   • You can only record one number in each digit's place.

   • When you roll two dice, the sum can never be a 1.

   • Zero is an important placeholder in a number.

10. Ask if any **questions** arose as a result of playing the game and record them on the "Further Investigations" chart. You can decide which ones to follow up on at a later time.

11. Tell students to respond to the following problem in their journals. First, have them draw the boxes for a two-digit number and a trash can.

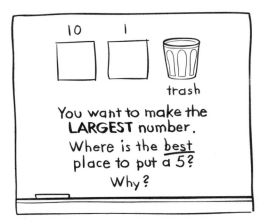

   a. Tell them you just got the sum of 5, and you have two more rolls to go. You want to make the LARGEST two-digit number possible.

   b. Ask for their advice on the best place to record the 5. Do they recommend putting it in the ten's place, the one's place, or in the trash?

   c. Have them explain why they chose that place.

12. After an appropriate amount of writing time, collect the journals. Reading their responses will provide an informal assessment of their understanding and help focus your instruction.

13. Read out loud the short story on page 40 entitled "Chapter 2: Zero's Family." You may want to write key words, big ideas, or numbers on the board as you read. Actively involve the students in the story. Encourage comments and discussion.

14. Continue to provide opportunities for students to play the game. **Be sure they have chances to make the lowest number possible as well as the highest number.** If they're recording the games in their journals, be sure they write HIGHEST or LOWEST at the top of their pages. Discuss the differences that creates in the game and encourage them to record their ideas in their journals.

Session 2:
Greater Than, Less Than, or Equal To?

■ What You Need

For the class:
- ❏ "What We Learned" chart from previous activities
- ❏ markers

For each pair of students:
- ❏ the set of base 10 materials from previous session
- ❏ 2 copies of the place value board from previous session
- ❏ 1 standard die (1–6)
- ❏ 1 special 0–3 die (as made and used in Activity 1)

For each student:
- ❏ mathematics journal

■ Getting Ready

1. Have the dice, base 10 materials, and place value boards used in the first session of this activity ready to distribute to partners.

2. Have journals ready to distribute.

■ Rollin' and Recordin'

1. Tell students that once again they are going to use dice to create numbers. On the board, draw lines for each of the digits in the number. For example, if you will create a three-digit number, draw three lines and label the digit's places as follows:

    100   10   1

    ___   ___   ___

2. Explain that as in the game Into the Trash It Goes! they will again add the sum of the numbers on two dice to determine what number to record in each digit's place. But this time they will use a different pair of dice—one 0–3 die and one standard 1–6 die.

3. Ask what is the smallest sum that can be made from the two dice. [1—from a 0 plus a 1.] Ask what's the largest sum. [9—from a 3 plus a 6.] Review all the other possible sums.

4. Tell students that in this game they **MUST** *record the number from right to left* (from the one's place to the hundred's). Point out that there is **NO** "trash can" to discard a number. Repeat that, unlike the earlier games, they cannot choose the place to record the number— they must start from the one's place and go to the left.

5. To demonstrate, roll the dice. Have students calculate the sum. [2 + 1.] Ask where you need to record this number. (Remind them again that this time there is no choice about where to record the number.)

The numbers given in brackets, such as 2 + 1, are just examples. You should substitute whatever numbers you and your student partner actually roll.

6. Select a student to come up to the board and record the number 3 (whatever number you actually rolled) in the one's place.

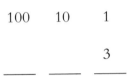

    100   10   1

                  3
    ____ ____ ____

7. Ask what place value should be filled next. [Tens.] Have a student roll the dice for you and determine the sum. [4 + 0.] Ask another student to record the 4 in the ten's place.

    100   10   1

            4   3
    ____ ____ ____

8. Now, have another student roll the dice to determine the number for the hundred's place. [3 + 3.] Have a volunteer record the number 6 in the hundred's place.

    100   10   1

      6   4   3
    ____ ____ ____

9. Have students say the number to a classmate first, and then have the class read it aloud.

■ Rollin' and Recordin' a Second Number

1. On the board, to the right side of the number that was just recorded, draw three lines and label the digit's places to create a second three-digit number.

100	10	1		100	10	1
6	4	3		___	___	___
___	___	___				

2. Roll the dice to determine the numbers for each of the digits in the second number. Have student volunteers roll the dice and other volunteers record the numbers. **Remember to start with the one's place.**

100	10	1		100	10	1
6	4	3		7	1	2
___	___	___		___	___	___

3. Select two students to build the two numbers with the base 10 materials on the place value boards.

4. Have the class compare the numbers. Which number is larger or greater? Which is smaller or lesser? [Though the numbers are not equal in this case, equality is the other possible relationship between the two numbers. They could be the same.]

■ Symbolic Notation

1. Write them on the board as you introduce or review the symbols for:

greater than   >

less than   <

equal to   =

Tool to remember symbols: The "greater than" symbol can be thought of as a "wide-open crocodile mouth" hungry to eat the larger number.

2. Emphasize that the symbol for "greater than" always has the widest side of the symbol closest to the larger of two numbers. The "point" on the symbol is always closest to the lesser or smaller of two numbers.

3. Have students determine which sign to write between the two numbers on the board. Be sure they compare the numbers in the order that they are recorded. Record the appropriate symbol.

6 4 3   <   7 1 2

4. Read the statement aloud with the class: "643 is less than 712."

5. Below 643 < 712, rewrite the two numbers in reverse order as follows:

already on board   6 4 3   <   7 1 2

now write   7 1 2   6 4 3

6. Ask students what symbol should go between the two numbers if they were in this second order. [Greater than.] Record the symbol as follows:

7 1 2   >   6 4 3

7. Read the statement aloud with the class: "712 is greater than 643."

8. Once more, focus their attention on the symbols for greater than and less than. Point out that, in each case, the open side of the symbol is closest to the larger number and the point is closer to the smaller number.

■ Rolling, Recording, and Comparing Numbers

1. Distribute the journals, then tell students that they will work with a partner to:

• Make two two- or three-digit numbers.

• Record the numbers in their journals.

• Compare the two numbers and record the correct symbol between them.

2. Demonstrate how this will work with an example. On the board, record a model for the two numbers:

100   10   1   100   10   1

____   ____   ____   ____   ____   ____

While this example may seem too much like the one just given, what you're modeling here is how to play the game with a partner as well as how to record the game in a journal.

3. Have them copy this in their journals. Select two students and record their names above the numbers:

Benjamin			Hana		
100	10	1	100	10	1
___	___	___	___	___	___

Again, use the sums of the actual numbers your students roll. This is just an example.

4. Hana goes first and rolls a sum of 7. Ask, "Which digit's place will the 7 be recorded in?" [Ones.] Record the number in the one's place for Hana's number. Have students record the number in their journals.

Benjamin			Hana		
100	10	1	100	10	1
___	___	___	___	___	7

5. Next, Benjamin rolls a sum of 4. Record the number in the one's place on Benjamin's side. The students do the same in their journals.

Benjamin			Hana		
100	10	1	100	10	1
___	___	4	___	___	7

6. Have students look at the one's digits. Which is greater, 4 or 7? [7.]

7. Ask where Hana will record the next digit. [Ten's place.] Hana rolls a sum of 1. Everyone records the 1 in Hana's ten's place.

Benjamin			Hana		
100	10	1	100	10	1
___	___	4	___	1	7

8. Benjamin rolls a sum of 5 and it is also recorded in his ten's place.

Benjamin			Hana		
100	10	1	100	10	1
___	5	4	___	1	7

9. Have students compare these two-digit numbers. Which is greater, 54 or 17? [54.]

10. Now the students roll the numbers for the hundred's place. Hana rolls a sum of 2 and Benjamin rolls a sum of 3.

Benjamin   Hana

100   10   1   100   10   1

___3_   _5_   _4___   ___2_   _1_   _7___

11. Have Hana and Benjamin each build their number with base 10 materials on their place value boards to compare them. **It is important to emphasize this step to your students.**

12. Ask, "Is Benjamin's number greater than, less than, or equal to Hana's number?" [Greater than.]

13. Record the symbol for greater than to state the relationship between the two numbers. Have students record the symbol in their journals.

100   10   1   100   10   1

___3_   _5_   _4___   >   ___2_   _1_   _7___

> Keep students focused on the comparison of the numbers. There are no winners or losers— the largest number is simply greater in value.

■ Partners Play Independently

1. As needed, review or answer questions about how to work together to create, record, and compare numbers. Remind students to record starting with the one's place.

2. Pair up students, and distribute dice and base 10 materials.

3. Circulate as they work. Check to make sure they build the numbers with base 10 materials to compare the magnitude, and that they use the symbolic notation accurately.

4. After students have finished working, focus their attention on the "What We Learned" chart. Record the symbolic notation and their definitions on the chart. Include an example of each.

$<$	is defined as less than	$5 < 10$
$>$	is defined as greater than	$10 > 5$
$=$	is defined as equal to	$10 = 10$ or $5 = 5$

5. Have students record these symbols and definitions in their journals.

6. Ask if there are any other things to record on the "What We Learned" chart.

■ Going Further

1. Presto Change-O Game

This fast-paced game gives students practice using the place value board and building numbers. It is best played before or at the end of a place value activity. Each student needs a place value board and base 10 materials.

a. Start by having students build a two-digit number such as 45. Say "Presto Change-O, 54." Students have to change the 45 to 54.

b. Now say "Presto Change-O, add one more ten." Ask what number is now on their board. [64.]

c. Continue along these line, providing practice building numbers. This is a great way to concretely practice the concept of one more and one less, as well as 10 more and 10 less.

2. Guess My Number

In this game, students guess a number based on a series of clues about the digits in the number. The first time you play, have students engage in the game without recording. Once they get the hang of it, they can record their guesses as the clues unfold.

a. Introduce the game by telling students you are thinking of a secret number and it has two digits—in the ten's place and the one's place.

Draw two lines on the board as follows:

_____   _____

Ask them how to label the digits, then label them.

10   1

_____   _____

b. Continue to provide clues for students to determine the number. For example, the following series of clues allows them to guess the number 45:

Clue 1: *It is an odd number.*
Have students review the definition of an odd number. [It cannot be divided into two equal whole numbers.] If the number is odd, what do they know about your secret number? [One's place can only be a 1, 3, 5, 7, or 9.]
Write the odd numbers in the one's place, as follows:

10   1

                 1, 3, 5, 7, 9
_____   _____

Clue 2: *You can get to the number by counting by 5s.*
Review skip-counting with 10s or 2s as necessary.
Skip-count by 5s. What do students know about your secret number now? [One's place can only be a 5.]
Erase the other numbers in the one's place.

10   1

                          5
_____   _____

Clue 3: *The digit in the one's place is greater than the digit in the ten's place.*
Have students explain what this means. [The digit in the ten's place is less than 5, so it can only be 1, 2, 3, or 4.]
Record the possible numbers for the ten's place.

10   1

1, 2, 3, 4   5
_____   _____

Clue 4: *The digit in the ten's place is even.*
Have students talk to a partner to see what numbers the ten's digit can be. [2 and 4.]
After someone explains to the class, *erase the 1 and 3.*

10   1

2, 4   5
_____   _____

Clue 5: *The digit in the ten's place is equal to 1 + 3.*
With this final clue, everyone knows the number in the ten's place is 4.
Erase the 2. The secret number is 45.

10	1
4	5

c. Here are some clues for additional two-digit and three-digit numbers.

Note: In the examples below, ★★ indicates the point at which the number can be guessed.

Secret Number is 50
Clue 1: The number is even.
Clue 2: The one's digit is less than the ten's digit.
Clue 3: The ten's digit is odd.
Clue 4: The sum of the digits is 5.
Clue 5: One of the digits equals the number of toes
　　　　on one foot. ★★
Clue 6: The number is half of 100.

Secret Number is 27
Clue 1: The number is odd.
Clue 2: The one's digit is greater than the ten's digit.
Clue 3: The ten's digit is even.
Clue 4: The sum of the digits is 9.
Clue 5: The ten's digit equals the number of eyes
　　　　on a person. ★★
Clue 6: The one's digit equals the number of sides on a triangle
　　　　plus the number of sides on a square.

Secret Number is 580
Clue 1: The number is even.
Clue 2: The ten's digit is greater than 5 and less than 9.
Clue 3: The hundred's digit is equal to the number of fingers on
　　　　one hand.
Clue 4: The sum of the digits is 13.
Clue 5: The ten's digit is equal to the number of legs
　　　　on two cats. ★★
Clue 6: Zero the Hero is one of the digits in the number.

We recommend having students play the game with two-digit numbers first before going to three-digit numbers **even if** they have experience with three-digit numbers.

Secret Number is 209

Clue 1: The number is odd.

Clue 2: The ten's digit is less than the one's digit and less than the hundred's digit.

Clue 3: The hundred's digit is an even number.

Clue 4: The one's digit is greater than the hundred's digit.

Clue 5: Zero the Hero is one of the digits in the number.

Clue 6: The sum of the digits is 11.

Clue 7: The one's digit is equal to the number of sides on a triangle plus the number of sides on a hexagon. ★★

Clue 8: If you divide the number of legs on a rabbit in half, it would equal the number in the hundred's place.

d. Students can also create clues for their own secret numbers and challenge their classmates to guess their numbers!

3. Literature Connections

Read the books *Even Steven and Odd Todd* by Kathryn Cristaldi and *Among the Odds & Evens: A Tale of Adventure* by Priscilla Turner. Both of these stories provide an opportunity to talk about even and odd numbers.

Chapter 2: Zero's Family

One day Zero was taking a walk in the Land of Numbers when the most amazing thing happened. She saw another Zero! The other Zero was younger, but definitely a Zero. Zero could hardly believe her eyes and gasped, "Who are you?"

The younger Zero said, "I'm a member of the family of Zeros."

You can imagine how excited Zero was! She took the young Zero by the hand and they ran together to the Queen of Numbers.

Since the Queen knew all things about numbers, she knew that there were many Zeros. And she knew there were many important things for Zeros to do in the Land of Numbers.

She called for all the numbers to gather round. Again, she asked the number 1 for help. Number 1 was happy to cooperate and stepped forward.

The Queen had 1 stand in front of her. Then she asked Zero to stand to the right of 1. Next, she asked the young Zero to stand to the right of Zero. Now the number they made was 100!

Amazing! They had grown from the 10s to numbers with three digits—the hundreds. This new number 100 was greater than all the two digit numbers.

The numbers 2, 3, 4, 5, 6, 7, 8, and 9 were amazed! They wanted to have two Zeros as their partners too.

With the help of the Queen they were able to make the numbers 200, 300, 400, 500, 600, 700, 800, and 900.

Zero became even more respected as an important number. In fact, some numbers were overheard calling Zero a Hero!

1s

ones

10s

tens

100s hundreds

10s tens

1s ones

Into the TRASH It Goes!

- **Roll** 2 dice.

- **Add** the numbers on the dice.

$$3 + 4 = 7$$

Circle your choice:

Will you roll for the **HIGHEST** or **lowest** number?

You may throw one sum in the trash!

If the sum is:
- **2–9**, write that **number** in a digit's place.
- **10, 11, 12**, write a **0** in a digit's place.

Player #1 ——
Roll and Record Your Number:

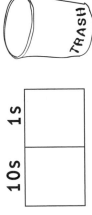

10s	1s

+

Player #2 ——
Roll and Record Your Number:

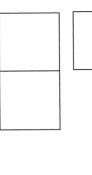

10s	1s

+

Into the TRASH It Goes!

- **Roll** 2 dice.
- **Add** the numbers on the dice.

3 + 4 = 7

Circle your choice:

Will you roll for the
HIGHEST or **lowest** number?

If the sum is:
- **2-9**, write that number in a digit's place.
- **10, 11, 12**, write a 0 in a digit's place.

You may throw one sum in the trash!

Player #1
Roll and Record Your Number:

100s	10s	1s

TRASH!

+

Player #2
Roll and Record Your Number:

100s	10s	1s

TRASH!

+

Overview

As students listen to action-filled number stories, they "hop" small toy frogs along a number line. They keep track of the movements of the frog by recording addition and subtraction equations that represent the movements.

In the number stories in Session 1, the final answer is always "Zero the Hero." The frog always starts at the number 0 and has adventures along the number line. After a series of moves, the frog returns to its "home," the number zero.

Number sentences (equations) are recorded to symbolically represent the movement of the frog throughout the story. In this first session, since the frog always begins on the zero and moves forward, students have an opportunity to see zero as the identity element of addition. A number plus zero $(5 + 0)$ or zero plus a number $(0 + 5)$ will always equal the number being added to zero $(5 + 0 = 0 + 5 = 5)$. In addition, students see that to return "home" to zero, a number must be subtracted from itself to equal zero $(5 - 5 = 0)$.

See "Background for the Teacher" on page 87 for more information on the identity element of addition.

In Session 2, the frog again moves along the number line according to a story. However, this time the answer at the end of the story (the final equation) is always the number 1 (*1's the One!*). Number sentences are recorded to keep track of the frog's hopping about with the final equation always equaling 1.

In Session 3, *Algebra in Action*, students encounter equations that begin on any number on the number line from 0 to 20 and end on a different number. They determine which direction the frog must move and how many jumps the frog must take.

Students solve for the missing addend or subtrahend by moving the frog along the number line. After solving each equation, students focus on the meaning of equality—that the computation on one side of the equation equals the number on the other side of the equal sign. For example, after solving and recording $7 + 5 = 12$, students also record a final equation, $12 = 12$.

See "Background for the Teacher" on page 87 for the vocabulary for addition and subtraction problems.

As students use the number line to solve equations, they **represent and analyze mathematical situations using algebraic symbols.** They tell the frog's movement story using numbers and symbols connecting a concrete representation of addition and subtraction to the abstract representation. Also, by having one set of stories begin at the number 0, the **identity element of addition** is introduced in an informal manner. **Number facts** are also reinforced (tying the Algebra standard together with the Number and Operations standard) as students solve the problems. The concept of an **unknown** in equations is introduced and the meaning and understanding of **equality** is deepened.

Session 1: The Answer Is Zero

■ What You Need

For the class:
- ❑ "What We Learned" chart from previous activities
- ❑ markers
- ❑ teacher read aloud: "Chapter 3: Zero's Home" (page 59)
- ❑ transparent tape

For each student:
- ❑ number line
- ❑ 1 small plastic frog, or other animal or marker
- ❑ mathematics journal

■ Getting Ready

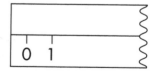

The unit measure between 0 and 1 is critical.

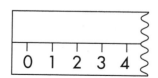

Subsequent numbers must be that same measure.

1. Decide how to obtain or make number lines for your students from the following **options:**

   a. Use sentence strips or similar strips of paper and guide your students in making their own number lines. Be sure students space the numbers an equal distance apart. The first unit measure is the distance from 0 to 1. Use that same distance to measure each subsequent number. (Adding machine tape can also be used, though it tends to curl up.)

   OR

   b. Duplicate a number line (page 60) for each student. Cut out the two strips and tape them together, carefully overlapping to get the distance between 10 and 11 correct.

   OR

c. Purchase number lines from the source listed on page 116.

2. Decide what small plastic animal or marker your students will use to move along the number line. Gather one for each student. A source for frogs is listed on page 116.

3. Read over the story "Chapter 3: Zero's Home" (page59) to familiarize yourself with it before reading it aloud to the class.

4. Have the journals available for students to use to record the number sentences derived from the stories told about the frog.

■ Home Sweet Home

1. Distribute a number line to each student. Have students locate various numbers on the number line to get familiar with it.

2. Tell students that a "frog" (or any animal you use) lives at the number 0 on the number line. Sometimes the frog hops to other numbers, but it always returns home to 0. Their job will be to help the frog get back home.

3. Distribute a frog to each student. Have them place their frogs on the 0.

4. Start with a story, such as:

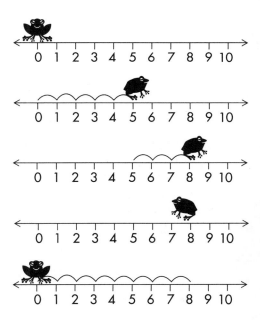

"One day the frog hopped to her favorite number 5."
Students hop the frog to the number 5.

"Then she took three hops to get to the pond."
Students hop the frog three times.
Ask: "What number is she at now?" [8.]

"After a swim, she decided to go home for a nap."
How many hops back does she have to go? [8.]
Say: "We have to go back eight hops to return to her home.
Turn the frog toward 0 and hop your frog home."

5. Continue making up other similar stories so the students have a chance to familiarize themselves with the number line. Be sure the stories have the frog moving in both directions—the positive direction (forward towards 20) and the negative (back towards 0).

■ Recording Froggie's Movements

1. Tell students that you want to record the story of the frog's movements. Instead of writing the words, you are going to use numbers and symbols to keep track of the frog.

2. As you tell another story, record the number sentences that represent the movements. For example, begin by saying:

   "On Sunday, Froggie woke up early."
   Ask: "Where is Froggie?" [On the number 0, her home.]

   "She decided to stretch her legs and hopped to the number 7."
   Have students move their frogs to the number 7.

   Ask: "Where did the frog start?" [0.]
   Write a 0 on the board.

   $$0$$

   Ask: "How far did she hop?" [Seven hops.]
   Add 7 to the 0.

   $$0 + 7$$

   Have students identify the "+" symbol.

   Ask: "Where is Froggie now?" [On the number 7.]
   Add the "=" symbol and 7 to complete the equation.

   $$0 + 7 = 7$$

   Have students read the equation. Tell them it's a number sentence.

   "The frog saw her friends ahead at the park. She wanted to leap and play with them."
   Ask what number the frog is on. [7.]
   Record a 7 below the first equation.

   $$0 + 7 = 7$$
   $$7$$

   Have students move the frog 2 leaps.
   Write a "+ 2" on the board next to the 7.

   $$0 + 7 = 7 \quad \text{first equation}$$
   $$7 + 2$$

   Ask students why you wrote "+2".
   Then ask: "What number is the frog on?" [9.]

Ask: "How can we write that to make an equation?"

$0 + 7 = 7$ first equation

$7 + 2 = 9$

Have the students read the completed equation and be sure they know the names of the + and = symbols.

"After the frog plays with her friends for a while, she gets hungry and wants to go home for a snack."
Ask: "How many hops does the frog have to take to get back to zero—her home?" [Nine hops.]

Ask how to record hopping backward toward zero. [Use a subtraction symbol.] Then record on the board as follows:

$0 + 7 = 7$ first equation

$7 + 2 = 9$ second equation

$9 - 9$ emphasize the subtraction symbol

Ask how to complete the third equation.

$0 + 7 = 7$ first equation

$7 + 2 = 9$ second equation

$9 - 9 = 0$ third equation;
                    add the = symbol and 0

Have the students read the completed equation.

3. Point out that these three equations are **number sentences** that tell the story of how Froggie moved. The frog made it home to **ZERO!**

■ More Hopping Around!

1. Tell similar stories and have students move their frogs along the number line according to the statements. Continue to record the number sentences for the class.

2. Have students record the number sentences in their journals to keep track of the movement of the frog in the stories.

3. Here is another story, and the equations that record the movement of the frog. Be sure to ask students how to record movements and to read equations along the way.

"One rainy day, Froggie took 6 hops FORWARD to get to her friend Frida's house."
$0 + 6 = 6$

*Start each story at the number 0. The final equation also always has **a zero for the answer** as the frog always ends there.*

"After they played for a while, they decided to go to the library. They took 4 hops FORWARD to get there."

$$0 + 6 = 6$$
$$\mathbf{6 + 4 = 10}$$

"Each frog chose a book. Then they went to get a fly sandwich at the Snack Shack. They take 2 hops BACK from the library."

$$0 + 6 = 6$$
$$6 + 4 = 10$$
$$\mathbf{10 - 2 = 8}$$

"Then they went back to Frida's house which was 2 hops BACK from the Snack Shack."

$$0 + 6 = 6$$
$$6 + 4 = 10$$
$$10 - 2 = 8$$
$$\mathbf{8 - 2\ = 6}$$

"It was time for Froggie to go home. She hopped BACK to her home. How many hops will she take?"

$$0 + 6 = 6$$
$$6 + 4 = 10$$
$$10 - 2 = 8$$
$$8 - 2 = 6$$
$$\mathbf{6}$$

"Finally, Froggie arrived BACK home and had her dinner."

$$0 + 6 = 6$$
$$6 + 4 = 10$$
$$10 - 2 = 8$$
$$8 - 2 = 6$$
$$\mathbf{6 - 6 = 0}$$

4. Encourage students to tell stories about the movement of the frog. Be sure that the numbers they use stay within the range of the number line. For example, the largest number of hops that the frog can take is 20 and that is only if the frog starts on the zero.

5. At the end of the session, ask students what they learned from using the number line with the frog. Record what they share on the "What We Learned" chart. Be sure to add the symbols for writing equations to the chart along with a definition of what they mean.

+ means ADD
− means SUBTRACT or TAKE AWAY
= means EQUAL

6. This activity may lead students to notice that zero plus a number equals that number and/or any number minus itself always equals zero. Add these to the chart as well.

$$0 + \text{Number} = \text{Same Number}$$
$$0 + 7 = 7$$
$$\text{Number} - \text{Same Number} = 0$$
$$7 - 7 = 0$$

By using 0 as a starting point, students are informally introduced to the identity property of addition. See page 90 for more information.

7. Have students record the new information that was added to the class chart in their journals. Collect the number lines and small plastic animals.

8. Read out loud the short story on page 59 entitled "Chapter 3: Zero's Home." You may want to write key words, big ideas, or numbers on the board as you read. Actively involve the students in the story. Encourage comments and discussion.

9. For homework, have students record a series of equations that represents one adventure of Froggie along the number line. They should be sure that Froggie **begins and ends** at the number **zero.**

Session 2: 1's the One!

■ What You Need

For the class:
- ❏ "What We Learned" chart from previous activities
- ❏ markers

For each student:
- ❏ number line
- ❏ 1 small plastic frog, or other animal or marker
- ❏ mathematics journal

■ Getting Ready

1. Gather the number lines used in Session 1.

2. Gather the small plastic animals (or markers) used to move along the number line in Session 1.

3. Have the journals available for students to record the number sentences from the stories told about the frog.

■ 1 is THE One!

1. Distribute the number lines and small animals used in Session 1. Have several students share the series of equations they did for homework. As students read their equations aloud, have their classmates move their frogs accordingly on their number lines.

2. Tell students that Froggie is now a year old and has moved into a new home—it is located at the number 1. Have them locate the 1 on the number line.

3. Froggie likes to move from the 1, but always returns to the number 1 at the end of her moves.

4. Record a 1 on the board. Have students place their frogs on the number 1.

5. Begin a new story, such as:

> *"Froggie decided to visit her old home, the number 0."*
>
> Ask what the frog needs to do to get to zero. [Move back 1 hop/number.] Ask how to record that move. [Subtract 1.] Record on the board as follows:
>
> 1 − 1

Ask: "Where is the frog now?" [At 0.]

Have students tell you how to complete the equation.
1 − 1 = 0

> *"Froggie wanted to go to the playground, so she took four hops forward to get there."*
>
> Have students hop their frogs forward four.
> Ask: "What number is she on now?" [4.]
> "How do we record that move?" [Froggie is at 0, so start with 0 then add 4. That equals 4.]
> 1 − 1 = 0
> **0 + 4 = 4**

Be sure all frogs are on the number 4.

> *"After playing for a while, Froggie wants to return to her new home—the number 1. What does the frog have to do?"*
>
> Write a partial equation on the board to represent your question.
> 1 − 1 = 0
> 0 + 4 = 4
> **4 ___ = 1**

Have students hop the frog to number 1.
Ask: "How many hops did the frog move?"
    "Did the frog move forward or backward?"

Ask how to record the movement in the equation. Using a student's guidance, fill in the missing piece:

$$1 - 1 = 0$$
$$0 + 4 = 4$$
$$\mathbf{4 - 3 = 1}$$

Have a student read the complete equation.

6. Have students record the three equations for this story in their journals.

7. Continue to give similar problems that are appropriate to your students' abilities. As you tell the story, have them record the equations to accompany it.

8. Have pairs of students make up a story and record the equations for it. Circulate as they work and ask questions to check for understanding.

9. At the end of the session, check to see if students want to add anything to the "What We Learned" chart. If you add to the chart, be sure they also record it in their journals.

> Note: *Remember to put the frog on* **the 1 to begin the story** *and to record a 1 as the first number in the equation. Also, the final equation always has a* **1 for the answer** *as the frog always ends there.*

Session 3: Algebra in Action

■ Getting Ready

1. Gather the number lines and small plastic animals or markers used in the previous sessions.

2. Have the journals available for students to record the number sentences from the stories told about the frog.

■ Solving Equations Using the Number Line

1. After your students understand how to use equations to represent the movements of the frog on the number line, provide a challenge.

2. Tell students that now the frog may *begin on any number* on the number line and may *end at any different number* on the number line.

3. Begin with an equation that has a starting point and an ending point. Students determine how many hops the frog needs to move either forward or backward to solve the equation.

4. Start with an example: Froggie was on the number 3 when she decided to skip to the number 8. Write the partial equation.

$$3 \rule{2cm}{0.4pt} = 8$$

5. Ask where the frog is located at the start of this equation. [3.] Have students place their frogs on the 3.

6. Ask what number the frog lands on after skipping. [8.]
Have students put one finger on the number 3 and keep it there, while with the other hand they skip their frogs to the 8.
Ask: "How many skips did the frog take?" [5.]
"Did the frog skip forward or backward?" [Forward.]
"Do we add or subtract?" [Add.]

7. Ask students what number needs to be added to the equation to make it equal. Select a volunteer to come to the board and fill in the operational sign and the number.

$$3 \quad \underline{+ \quad 5} \quad = 8$$

Have students read the equation to each other.

8. Take this opportunity to introduce the full meaning of equality. Below the equation write:

$$3 \quad \underline{+ \quad 5} \quad = 8$$

$$8 = 8$$

9. Ask students to read the equation "8 = 8." Have them discuss with a partner what that equation means. Is it a true statement? Why or why not? Challenge them to explain their thinking to the class.

■ This Is Algebra!

1. Explain to your students that they solved an equation. There was a missing number and operation needed to make the equation complete! Both sides of an equation are equal—the quantity on each side is the same. Let the students know that when they figured out what the missing number was, they solved the equation.

2. Tell students that when they find the missing number in the equation **they are doing algebra!** Ask if anyone has ever heard of algebra. Listen to what they have heard about it.

3. Provide another equation with a missing number, such as:

7 – ____ = 5

4. Have students read the equation aloud. Explain that the blank represents a missing number. It is called an **unknown** (or a **variable**). The unknown can be represented by a blank or with a **symbol, such as a ?—or a star—or a letter.** The missing number will make the equation an equality.

5. Demonstrate how to use a symbol for the variable. Any symbol can be used to represent the missing number. For example, using the asterisk or star symbol (★) as the unknown:

7 – ★ = 5

6. Have students solve the equation with the help of their number lines. Put the frog on number 7, then put one finger on 7, and with the other hand, hop the frog to the 5.
Ask: "How many hops did it take?" [2.]
"Did the frog hop forward or backward?" [Backward.]
"Do we add or subtract?" [Subtract.]

7. Finally, substitute in the answer to see if the equation is true.

7 – ★ = 5
7 – **2** = 5
      5 = 5

The ★ is equal to 2.   ★ = 2.

8. Provide another equation for students to solve with a partner. Have them record the equation in their journals and use the frogs and their number lines to solve it.

9. Have students explain the solution to the problem. Check that students record all steps of the solution **including the equality.** For example, if the equation you pose is:

6 + ★ = 10

The solution is ★ = 4

Substitute in the value for ★ and prove the equality.

$$6 + \mathbf{4} = 10$$
$$10 = 10$$

An understanding of equality
provides a foundation for solving
equations. It allows one to
determine the number or
numbers that will make the
equation a true statement.

10. Provide additional problems for your student to solve. You may want to vary the difficulty of the problems and let students self-select the ones they want to solve. In that way, they will work at their ability levels.

11. Circulate as they work and assist students as needed. This provides an opportunity to informally assess their understanding of the concepts presented as well as number facts.

12. At the end of the session, ask students if they want to add anything to the "What We Learned" chart. If anything new is added, be sure they record it in their journals.

■ Going Further

1. Solve This! Story Problems
Have students write story problems that have an unknown. Before they begin, brainstorm some of the words they will need to write coherent problems. Don't worry about where they place the unknown in their equations. After you review the problems, select a student to pose her problem to the class. Provide time for the class to solve the problem. Have a student come to the board to explain the solution.

2. Literature Connections
The following five books provide a variety of representations and contexts for writing and solving equations. (See full annotations on pages 119–121.)

- *12 Ways to Get to 11* by Eve Merriam
- *Mission: Addition* by Loreen Leedy
- *Safari Park* by Stuart J. Murphy
- *Sea Sums* by Joy Hulme
- *Ten Friends* by Bruce Goldstone

Chapter 3: Zero's Home

The Queen of Numbers decided that all the numbers needed their own places to call their homes.

She decided to place their homes in a line. The Queen started with Zero. Once Zero was placed, she left a space and placed the number 1. Then the Queen measured the same spacing distance again and placed number 2. She kept placing numbers in the same way until she got to 100. After 100, the Queen needed a rest!

After her rest, the Queen looked at the line of numbers and felt quite pleased with herself. She decided to have some fun and visit some numbers by hopping along the line. The Queen started at Zero's home and hopped nine times and landed on the number 9, of course.

Then, from there, she decided to skip and she skipped five more times forward. The Queen had so much fun skipping, she forgot to add the numbers as she skipped.

Luckily, she remembered that 9 is the hungriest of all numbers. Nine always wants to "eat" one more and grow to 10. When 9 gets together with another number, he nibbles one away from that number and he becomes a 10. So, the other number shrinks by one. Because she'd started from 9, it became a 10, and her five skips became four. She added 10 and 4 and figured out she was on the number 14.

Then the Queen decided to jump by 2s. From the 14, she long-jumped to 16, then 18, 20, 22, 24, 26, 28, and ended on 30.

After all this hop-skip-and-jumping along the number line, the Queen was tired. She decided to walk back to Zero's home. So, she went 30 steps back. As she walked she thought: 30 minus 30 is Zero!

Zero had just made a pot of mint tea and was happy to serve the Queen a cup. So, the Queen relaxed for the rest of the afternoon with her good pal, Zero.

Number Line

```
0 — 
1 — 
2 — 
3 — 
4 — 
5 — 
6 — 
7 — 
8 — 
9 — 
10 — 
```

```
11 — 
12 — 
13 — 
14 — 
15 — 
16 — 
17 — 
18 — 
19 — 
20 — 
```

Overview

In this culminating activity, with two sessions, students apply what they've learned in prior sessions to generate equations that have an "unknown" (a missing number). They solve for the unknown as well as create stories for each equation. The location of the unknown can be placed in different positions in the equation to give students experience with many types of problems. Students begin by making a mini-book out of a single sheet of paper to record their equations and then create stories that go with them.

In the first mini-book, students use the sum of dice to generate the number for the start of an equation and the solution to that equation. The unknown is placed between those two numbers. Then students determine which operation—addition or subtraction—and what number will make the equation equal. As necessary, concrete materials and/or number lines assist in the problem solving and help make connections to the symbolic representation. After solving the equations, students create story problems to accompany their equations.

See "Background for the Teacher" on page 87 for more information about problem types.

Following their experiences solving for the unknown in the first session, in Session 2, More Equations to Solve, the unknown can be placed in other locations of the equation. To practice addition and/or subtraction facts, the unknown can be the solution to an equation. For a challenge, the unknown can be put at the start of the equation! Also, larger numbers can be used to tailor the problems to the skill levels of your students. For example, students can generate two-digit numbers to practice addition and subtraction with regrouping.

The activity provides opportunities to create equations with the support of concrete materials and number lines. In this way, the symbolic notation is understood and students gain facility at conventional notation. As problem types are introduced, students see that an unknown can be placed in various locations in equations. In addition, as they record equations, the rolls of the dice are likely to include zero as the identity element of addition. This final activity also provides opportunities to discuss strategies for solving addition and subtraction problems.

Session 1: What's Missing?

■ What You Need

For the class:
- ❑ "What We Learned" chart from previous activities
- ❑ markers
- ❑ teacher read aloud: "Chapter 4: Number Tricks" (page 76)
- ❑ extra two-sided copies of the **What's Missing?** mini-book template (pages 78–79)

For each pair of students:
- ❑ dice (see "Getting Ready" #3)
- ❑ number line
- ❑ *(optional)* counters

For each student:
- ❑ 1 two-sided copy of the **What's Missing?** mini-book template (pages 78–79)
- ❑ scissors
- ❑ mathematics journal

■ Getting Ready

1. Make one copy of the **What's Missing?** mini-book (pages 78–79) for each student and at least four additional copies for you to use. Copy the two pages of the template back-to-back for correct construction of the book.

2. Practice making the mini-book before demonstrating it to your students. Step-by-step instructions are described on pages 65–66. You will need **two pre-made** books to model how to play the game.

3. Decide on which dice your students will use to generate numbers. Consider their skills and abilities, and choose the dice based on the magnitude of the numbers you'd like your students to use. For example:

   • Use a 0–3 die and a standard die for numbers 1–9.

   • Use two standard dice for numbers 2–12.

   • Use a 0–3 die and two standard dice for numbers 2–15.

   • Use three standard dice for numbers 3–18.

Rather than dice, you may want to use spinners with numbers appropriate for your students' skills. For example, one spinner can be 0–5 and another 5–10. Students can use just one or a combination of the two.

- Use die of two different colors to make 2-digit numbers, one color for 10s, the other for 1s.

- Use icosahedron dice (20-sided; numbers 0-9 twice) to roll all single digit numbers, 0–9.

4. Have the copies of the mini-book templates and scissors ready to demonstrate how to make the mini-book for the students. Also have available your two pre-made books and the students' journals.

5. Have dice ready to distribute and have number lines available for students to solve equations. (Counters are optional.)

6. Read over the story "Chapter 4: Number Tricks" (page 76) to familiarize yourself with it before reading it out loud to the class.

■ Making the Mini-Book

1. Show students the book you made and let them know that they are going to make a book just like yours. After their books are made, they will use them to record equations and write stories to go with the equations.

2. Unfold your book into the original rectangular sheet of paper you began with. Tell students you're going to walk them through the process of making a book.

3. Distribute scissors and a copy of the mini-book template to each student. Ask students to stay at your pace—they should do each step, one at a time, after you demonstrate what to do.

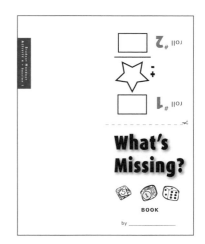

4. Have them locate the small illustration of a pair of scissors on the paper. Next, have them look at the dotted line next to the scissors. Ask them to notice that the dotted line does not go across the entire paper!

5. Demonstrate how to cut along the dotted line and STOP when you have cut half way across the width of the paper. Have students cut along the dotted line.

6. Have students look at both sides of the paper and note the differences on each side. Locate the side of the paper that has two equations and two titles, "My Story Problem."

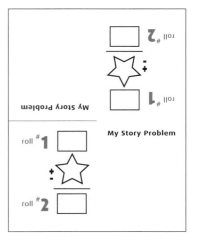

7. Lay that side of the paper FACE UP—it will look like this:

8. Tell students they will FOLD the paper in half, lengthwise. Have students make that fold. The result of this fold is a long, narrow white rectangle that looks like this:

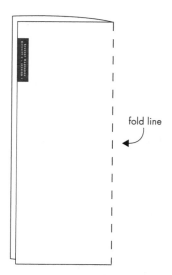

fold line

9. Flip the paper over, then fold the long rectangle in half across the width. Have students do the same. The steps of the process look like this:

fold down

10. Congratulate the students. They've just made a mini-book!

11. Tell students to write their name on the cover of their books and set them aside.

■ Rolling and Recording

1. Gather students in an area away from their desks to avoid distraction as you demonstrate how to fill their books. Have the dice, two pre-made books, and number lines ready to use.

2. Select a student partner to play with you. Each of you takes one of the pre-made books and writes your name on the cover.

3. Open the book and go over the first page with the students. Be sure they note where the "roll #1" box and "roll #2" box are positioned, as well as where the star is located.

4. Have your partner begin by rolling the dice and adding together the numbers rolled. She records the sum of the dice in the box next to "roll #1."

5. Next, you roll the dice and record the sum of your dice in the "roll #1" box in your book.

6. Follow the same process for "roll #2." Be sure students notice that roll #2 is recorded as the *solution* to the equation!

■ Solving

1. Focus on the equation in your book. For example, if you had a 9 for roll #1 and a 5 for roll #2 use a number line and place one finger on 9, then locate the 5. Ask students to determine if you need to add or subtract to get from 9 to 5. [Subtract.]

2. Circle the operation that you will use. [Subtraction sign.]

3. Read the equation, "Nine minus some number is equal to five." Tell students the star represents the number that is missing. Let them know it is called an ***unknown***.

4. Ask students to work with a partner to determine what number the star needs to equal to solve this equation. As appropriate for your students' skills and abilities, they can use a number line (or optionally, counters) to help calculate the missing number.

5. After students have had some time to work on the problem, ask a volunteer to tell you the number they came up with. Record the value inside the star, and read the completed equation to the class,

Teacher's Book

Teacher's Book

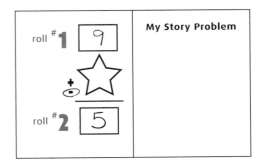

Teacher's Book

Teacher's Book

"Nine minus four equals five." Check that the class agrees the equation is accurate.

6. Have your partner read the information in her equation to determine what operation she will need to use to solve her equation. Circle the operation.

7. Have your partner find the unknown for her equation and read it to the class. Check to make sure they agree that her equation is accurate when she fills in her value for the star.

8. Review how to complete the equations in their books. Point out the other page with "My Story Problem" written at the top. Tell students they will complete that part **after** they make their equations.

■ Recording and Solving Equations

1. Have partners go to their work areas and help each other complete the **three** equations in their books. Remind them that number lines are available to assist with the calculations. (Counters are optional.)

2. Circulate as students work and assist as necessary.

3. If some pairs finish quickly, have them make another book and generate additional equations.

■ Writing Story Problems

1. When most students have completed their equations, focus the class for a discussion on how to write story problems.

2. Start by going back to your original equation, "9 − 4 = 5." Ask partners to tell each other a story that could go with your equation.

3. Listen to a few stories. Identify a few of the action words students use to tell what happened in their stories.

4. As a group, brainstorm words that are used in story problems. Record these words on the "What We Learned" chart so students can refer to them as they write their own story problems.

5. Be sure to tell stories for **both** addition and subtraction and generate words for both types of story problems. The list is likely to include such words as:

Story Problem Words

add	added to
all gone	all together
another	
ate	
bought	
came along	
flew away	
gave	gave away
get	got
had	have
how many less	how many more
joined	
left	
less	less than
lose	lost
minus	
more	more than
need	
no more	
none	none left
plus	
subtract	
take away	
threw away	
took	took away
used	used up

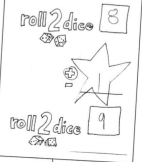

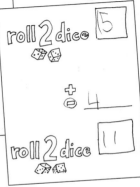

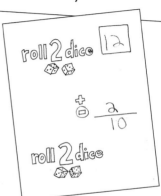

6. Have students record these key words in their journals.

7. Make sure students realize that there's no separate "My Story Problem" page for the third equation, so they'll write that story problem in their journals.

8. Have students write stories for their equations. Alternatively, have them write them at another class time or for homework.

9. Read out loud the short story on page 76 entitled "Chapter 4: Number Tricks." You may want to write key words, big ideas, or numbers on the board as you read. Actively involve the students in the story. Encourage comments and discussion.

Session 2: More Equations to Solve

■ What You Need

For the class:
- ❑ "What We Learned" chart from previous activities
- ❑ markers
- ❑ teacher read aloud: "Chapter 5: One Last Trick Featuring Zero" (page 77)
- ❑ extra two-sided copies of the mini-book template you've chosen

For each pair of students:
- ❑ dice (see "Getting Ready" #5)
- ❑ number line
- ❑ *(optional)* counters

For each student:
- ❑ 1 two-sided copy of the **What's Missing? Find the Result** or **Find the Start** mini-book template (pages 80–81 or 82–83)
- ❑ scissors
- ❑ mathematics journal

■ Getting Ready

or

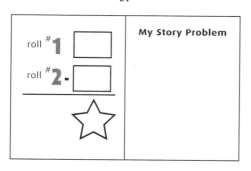

1. Based upon your students' skills and abilities, vary the problem types. The level of difficulty can also be changed by including two-digit numbers and regrouping.

2. Based on the information below, think about which mini-book template you'll copy for students. The following are examples of two problem types:

   Result Unknown Books
   These books support learning number facts. Consider the operation (addition or subtraction) for the book. If you choose to use subtraction, be sure the number for roll #1 *will always be greater than or equal to* the number for roll #2. To accomplish this, you could, for example, use two dice for roll #1 and use the two numbers rolled to make a two-digit number. Then use one icosahedron (20 sided) die to generate the lesser numbers 0 through 9 for roll #2.

Start Unknown Books (Second Grade Challenge!)

This is a more challenging type of equation. Since the unknown is in the first position, there's nothing for students to use as an "anchor" in their problem solving. For this reason, it is highly recommended that students use counters to help solve this type of problem. You may want to start with addition problems, and as students are able proceed to subtraction.

• Start Unknown Addition Problem

Roll *one die* to determine the value of roll #1 and record the number in the equation. Use *the sum of two or more dice* to determine the value of roll #2 and record the number. This is to be sure roll #2 is always greater than or equal to roll #1. It is important that roll #2 be greater because another number—the unknown—is being added to roll #1. Build the numbers with counters. Compare the numbers. Determine how much needs to be added to roll #1 to equal roll #2.

For example, let roll #1 = 6 and roll #2 = 9.

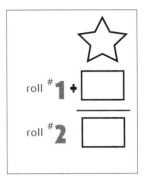

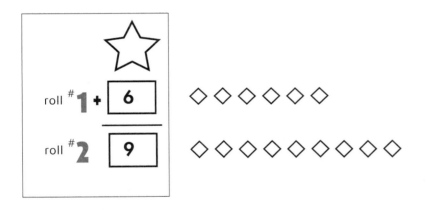

Have students compare the two numbers concretely to see that 9 is three more than 6. The unknown number is 3.

Additional Support to Solve Start Unknown Problems

Students may recognize this comparison of numbers from graphing situations. You may want to create a two-column graph to provide a context for the comparison. For example, graph a handful of blue and yellow cubes.

blue

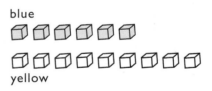

yellow

Have students make comparison statements about the graph and connect their statements to equations.

For more information on graphing, see the GEMS guide Treasure Boxes. *It contains an entire activity devoted to graphing.*

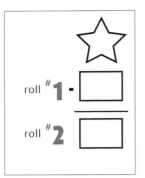

• Start Unknown Subtraction Problem
Roll two dice and use the sum as the value of roll #1. Record the number in the equation. Roll two dice again and use the sum as the value of roll #2. Record the number in the equation. (Unlike result unknown subtraction problems, here roll #1 does not have to be greater than roll #2.)

For example, let roll #1 = 7 and roll #2 = 5.

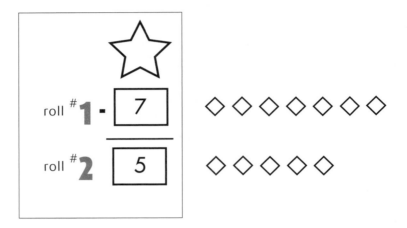

In this case, you start with some UNKNOWN number, then take 7 from that number and 5 remains. Build the two known numbers with counters, then *combine* and count the total. Reenact the subtraction from the total number and check that the numbers correspond. [When you create a group of 12 then take away 7, you *will* have 5 remaining.]

3. Decide which problem type you will have your students work with. Here are the types that have been suggested:

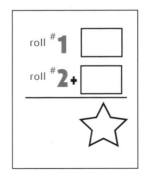   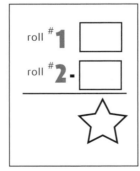   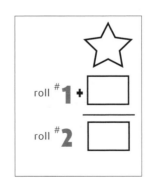   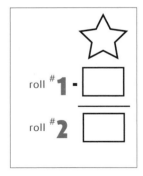

Result Unknown   *Start Unknown*

Also decide the operation (addition or subtraction) you'll use and write it in each equation. Then make one copy per student of *either* the **What's Missing? Find the Result** (pages 80–81) or the **What's**

Missing? Find the Start (pages 82–83) mini-book template. Be sure to copy the two pages of the template back-to-back.

4. The directions for making the book are the same. If you feel your students still need guidance on the steps in making the book, have an extra copy for that purpose. In addition, make two books so that you can demonstrate how to complete the new version of the What's Missing? mini-book.

5. As in the first session, decide which dice your students will use to generate numbers. See step 3 of the "Getting Ready" of Session 1. Alternatively, you can have students use spinners.

6. Gather scissors, dice, two pre-made books, and number lines and/or counting materials.

7. Read over the story "Chapter 5: One Last Trick Featuring Zero" (page 77) to familiarize yourself with it before reading it out loud to the class.

■ Making and Using New Books

1. Distribute scissors and a copy of the new version of the mini-book to each student. Have students make a new book. When they are done, have them compare this book to the original one they completed.

2. Guide students to the location of the unknown in this new book. Ask if they know what they will be doing to find the unknown.

3. Select a partner to demonstrate how to complete the equations in the book. Begin by writing your names on the covers of your books. Take your first roll and record the sum of the dice in the box for roll #1. Have your partner do the same. Take a second roll and record the sum in the box for roll #2. Have your partner do the same.

4. Ask the students how to solve for the unknown in the equations. Provide a number line and, as necessary, counting materials to support them in their explanations.

5. Record the appropriate number for the unknown in the star in each book.

6. Review with the students how to complete the equations in the book. Organize the students into pairs, distribute the dice, then have students generate and solve equations.

7. When they have completed the three equations in their books, have them write story problems for each one. Remind students to put the story for the third equation in their journals.

8. Read out loud the short story on page 77 entitled "Chapter 5: One Last Trick Featuring Zero." You may want to write key words, big ideas, or numbers on the board as you read. Actively involve the students in the story. Encourage comments and discussion.

■ Going Further

1. More Missing Numbers

Continue to provide opportunities for students to solve for unknowns in equations. You may want them to make several books with the same problem type for practice. Intersperse practice over time so they retain their skills.

2. Zero the Hero's Special Role in Addition Equations

- Have students look through their books for addition equations with ZERO the HERO in them. Ask what they notice about all of the equations. Remind them about the number line activity when Froggie "lived" at the number 0 (Activity 3, Session 1).

- Reemphasize ZERO the HERO's special role. You can add zero to any number and zero will NOT change the value of that number. Zero is called the IDENTITY ELEMENT of ADDITION. The number's identity or value does not change.

- If you have not already recorded this information on the "What We Learned" chart, add it now.

$$0 + \text{Number} = \text{Same Number}$$
$$\text{Number} + 0 = \text{Same Number}$$

3. Zero's Performance Piece

Look over the poem on the next page and decide whether to read all or part of it to the class. Alternatively, students might like to recite it. You could even use this poem as an inspiration for students to write a poem of their own!

4. More Number Tricks

After reading the short story on number tricks, have students think of additional tricks or strategies to do addition and subtraction computations. Provide time for students to share their strategies. See "Background for the Teacher" on page 87 for additional computational strategies you may want to introduce to your students.

A Performance Piece by Zero the Hero

I'm Zero the Hero and I'm way cool
You may think I'm nothing but don't be fooled
I can take any number and change it fast
As a place value holder I'm unsurpassed
Take any whole number, any old one
Put me to the right of it and watch the fun
Say it's a five then just add me
You get ten times more—a big fifty
Put another zero after that one
You get five hundred a very fine sum
And that's not all that I can do
I'm Zero the Hero and I'm way cool!

Without my power, may I say modestly
Our base 10 system just could not be
In fact my invention made math as we know it
It would not be the same with no way to show it
When you had ten apples then took ten away
I became the symbol for what remained
Then lo and behold as algebra grew
Folks found out more things I could do
There's positive numbers and negative too
But who's in between them—Zero that's who
Zero the Hero is right on that line
Between plus and minus I'm the road sign

Now all other numbers are special too
I need them to do the things I can do
In Spanish they praise "Numero Uno"
But they also could shout "Viva por Cero!"
I'm powerful, versatile, my talents are many
Though all by myself I just haven't any
But put me together, add subtract multiply
Even divide and you'll soon figure out why
I'm Zero the Hero and I bow to your cheers
And remind you a thing can be more than appears
Learn all about me—a handy math tool
I'm Zero the Hero and I'm way cool!

There are 36 lines when this poem is all done
But if you take them away there will be none!

Chapter 4: Number Tricks

The Queen of Numbers knew all about numbers. She loved to add numbers—especially doubles. Her favorite double was 8 + 8.

If she added two numbers that were not doubles, she had a few tricks up her sleeve. For example, if she added 6 + 7, she would think of 7 as 6 + 1. Since she knew 6 + 6 equals 12, just adding one more makes 13. It goes like this: 6 + 7 = 6 + 6 + 1 = 12 + 1 = 13.

At other times she liked to make 10s, because when you add 10 to a single digit number, the addition is so easy! For example, if the Queen wanted to add 6 + 8, first she would identify the largest number. In this case that's the number 8. Next, she would figure out the number that needed to be added to 8 to equal 10. Of course, being the Queen of Numbers she knew 8 + 2 = 10.

Since she needed to add 2 to 8 to make 10, she would rewrite 6 as 4 + 2. Then all she had to do was add 4 + 10 and get 14!

$$6 + 8 =$$
$$4 + 2 + 8 =$$
$$4 + 10 = 14!$$

The Queen knows lots of other number tricks. But she doesn't like to give them all away. She likes other number lovers to figure out some tricks of their own!

If you know any, send them in for her to try out!

Note to Teachers:
As you read this story, be sure to record the equations on the board as you go along. Then students can visually see how the number tricks work!

Chapter 5: One Last Trick Featuring Zero

The Queen of Numbers loved all of your ideas about how to add and subtract numbers.

She decided to share one more amazing thing about what Zero can do. But you have to promise not to tell anyone.

When you multiply, you add the number over and over a certain number of times. For example, if you have 4 x 2 that is the same as adding 2 four times—2 + 2 + 2 + 2. It's the same as moving along the number line by 2s four times. Some people call this "skip counting."

However, if you multiply a number by 0, the answer is always 0! It's an amazing thing to think about. Suppose you have the problem, "What is one million times 0?" You know the answer in a flash…it is ZERO!

Remember how, in addition, when you add 0 to a number, it's like doing nothing at all to a number? You can say: 0 plus any number equals that number.

But now, in multiplication, when Zero gets involved, Zero is the answer! Zero times any number equals Zero!

It's amazing what one number can do, isn't it? And that's only just the start of it! In many ways and places, Zero the Hero can make a very big difference. Zero the Hero, round like the Sun, helps us see math really is fun!

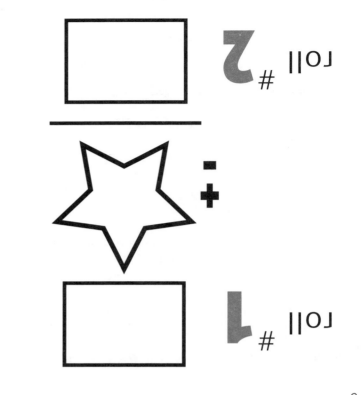

roll #2

roll #1

✂

What's Missing?

BOOK

by _____

roll #2

−
+

roll #1

My Story Problem

My Story Problem

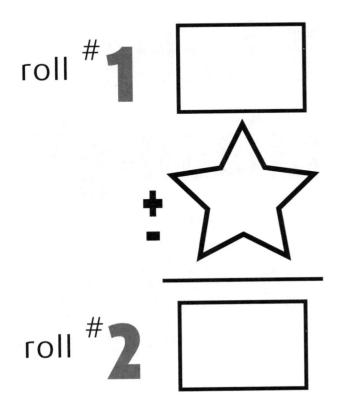

roll #1

+
−

roll #2

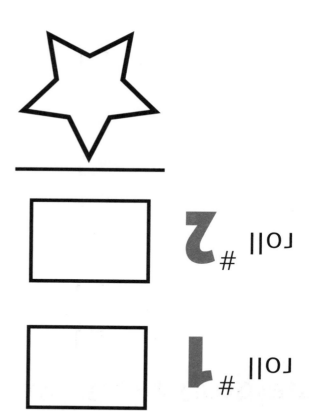

roll #2

roll #1

✂ — — — — — — —

What's Missing?

Find the Result

BOOK

by _____

My Story Problem

roll #**1**

roll #**2**

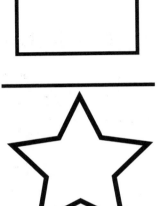

My Story Problem

roll #**1**

roll #**2**

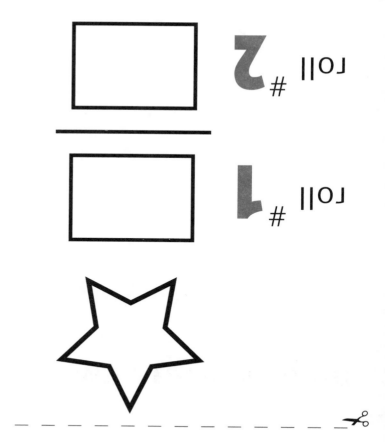

roll #1

roll #2

What's Missing?

Find the Start

BOOK

by _____

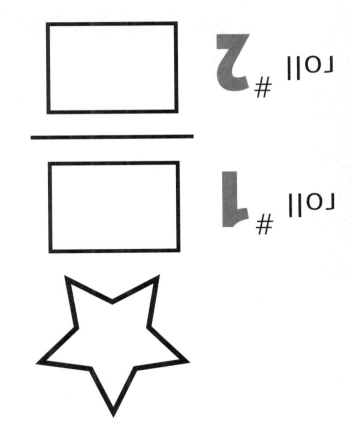

My Story Problem

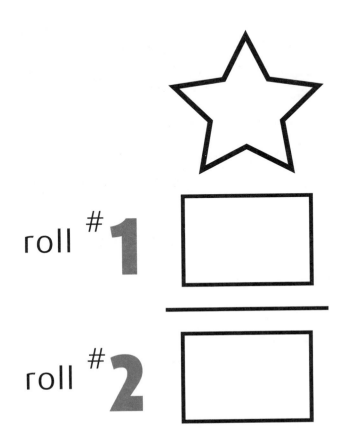

roll #**1**

roll #**2**

1. Journal Prompts

• Why do you think zero is called a hero? What is so special about zero?

• Is Zero the Hero an important number? Explain why it is or is not important.

• Do you think Zero the Hero is an ODD or an EVEN number? Explain your thinking.

2. Zero the Hero Illustrated

Use the picture frames on page 85 and have students draw caricatures of Zero the Hero. Post their Zero the Hero pictures around your school site with an interesting or thought-provoking question or comment about zero.

3. Literature Connections

There are two exceptional books about the number 0 that serve as a wonderful culmination and review of all that the students learned in the unit. These books are *Zero is Not Nothing* by Mindel and Harry Sitomer and *Zero: Is It Something? Is It Nothing?* by Claudia Zaslavsky. Look for both books in the children's non-fiction section of most libraries. See page 119 for more information on these books.

4. More Stories About Zero the Hero

Invite your students to write down and read out loud to the class their own stories about Zero the Hero.

Zero the Hero

by _____

Zero the Hero

by _____

Zero the Hero

by _____

Zero the Hero

by _____

BACKGROUND FOR THE TEACHER

This section is designed to serve as a resource on the algebraic concepts presented in this unit, and can help you prepare to teach the activities. *It's not intended to be read aloud to students or copied for their use.* It may, however, have the answers to some of the questions your students pose. These questions can provide insight into different levels of prior knowledge and misconceptions about algebra.

What is Algebra?

Algebra is essentially generalized arithmetic. It expresses the universal validity of certain statements in mathematics—especially those about numbers—by the use of symbols.

What is Algebraic Reasoning?

For students in grades one and two, algebraic reasoning includes developing an understanding of the following:

- the meanings of equality and inequality

- how to represent relationships as equations

- how to use symbols to represent a phenomenon

- how the base 10 computational system works for addition and subtraction

- how to solve equations with an unknown

- the role of zero in addition

- the role of zero in base 10 system

Algebraic reasoning is the process of explaining the rationale behind computations and solutions. Algebraic reasoning takes students beyond isolated computational exercises into understanding why we add and subtract as well as how the two operations are related. Algebraic reasoning lays the foundation for formal algebra.

The Vocabulary of Algebra

As with any subject, there are words essential to algebra that need definition. The following short list provides definitions for the terminology used in this unit.

Algebraic Expression: An algebraic expression is a mathematical phrase that includes one or more of the following: a constant (a quantity that remains the same), a variable (a value that changes), and an operation symbol. Just as a word phrase is not a sentence, an algebraic expression is not an equation. The following examples illustrate the difference:

Algebraic Expressions	*Equations*
12 (constant)	$12 = 12$ or $y = 12$
$8 + \star$	$8 + \star = 15$
$10 - x$	$y = 10 - x$

Equation: An equation is a mathematical statement that two expressions have equal value. For example, $5 = 5$; $7 + 2 = 9$; $6 + 4 = 5 + 5$; and $6 \cdot n = 30$.

Inequality: An inequality is a mathematical statement whose two expressions are not equal. For instance, $3 \neq 4$; $19 \neq 9 + 9$; and $6 + 7 \neq 10 + 4$. The mathematical symbols that define the inequalities are as follows:

$<$	less than	$3 < 4$	$y - 1 < 4$
$\leq$	less than or equal to	$6 \leq 6$	$y + 0 \leq 6$
$>$	greater than	$19 > 9$	$x + 6 > 18$
$\geq$	greater than or equal to	$15 \geq 15$	$x - 9 \geq 15$

Variable: Refers to a quantity that changes (as the word, *vary*, suggests) or that can have a range of possible values. For example, the variable z can be used to represent the total number of sides on triangles: $z = 3 \cdot$ number of triangles. If you have five triangles, then $z = 3 \cdot 5 = 15$ sides.

Single variables can also represent an unknown in an equation, rather than quantities that change. For example, $7 + n = 11$. In this case, when $n = 4$, the equation is a true statement. However, other values can be substituted resulting in an inequality.

Whole Numbers: In this unit, whole numbers are used in all activities. A whole number is all positive natural numbers and the number zero: 0, 1, 2, 3… The *natural or counting numbers* is a subset of whole numbers that start at the number one: 1, 2, 3…

In later grades students will learn about the other parts of the number system. *Real numbers* include the set of all rational and irrational numbers. Real numbers can be represented on a number line, with irrational numbers being approximated. The set of real number is infinite and includes the following numbers:

- *Integers:* negative and positive whole numbers: $-2, -1, 0, 1, 2…$

- *Rational Numbers* are numbers that can be expressed as a fraction or ratio, $\frac{a}{b}$ where $b \neq 0$. For example, $\frac{2}{1}$ (which equals 2); $\frac{3}{4}$; $\frac{-5}{15}$; .18 (fractional equivalent is $\frac{18}{100}$); etc.

- *Irrational Numbers:* numbers that cannot be represented by a fraction or ratio that have a terminating decimal. For example, pi ($\frac{22}{7}$ or 3.14…); square root of 2; $-2.236…$. These numbers can be approximated and situated on the number line.

This Venn diagram organizes the real number system:

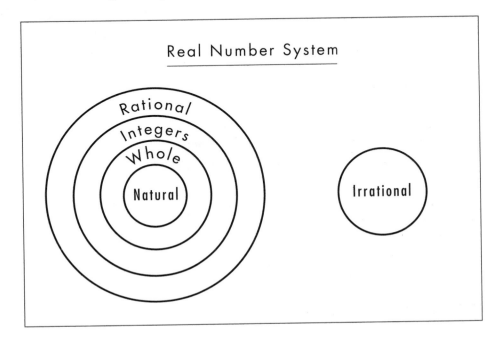

Real Number System

Rational
Integers
Whole
Natural

Irrational

The Vocabulary of Addition and Subtraction

The following equations review the vocabulary of the various parts of equations for the two computational operations in this unit.

Addition Equation: Addend + Addend = Sum

> *Addend*: any number being added to a number(s) to produce a sum.
> *Sum*: the total; the result of adding at least two numbers together.

Subtraction Equation: Minuend − Subtrahend = Difference

> *Minuend*: the number you subtract from.
> *Subtrahend*: the number being subtracted.
> *Difference*: the amount remaining after a quantity is subtracted from another quantity.

The terminology for subtraction isn't generally used in mathematics, and isn't important to emphasize.

Properties of Numbers and Operations

The following properties are basic laws of operations for our number system. Primary students first encounter these laws informally and gain an intuitive understanding of them through concrete examples. In this unit, students may have the opportunity to "name" and define the Identity Element of Addition.

Identity Element of Addition

An identity element is a number that combines with any other number **in any order** without changing the original number. There are two identity elements, one for addition and one for multiplication (which is beyond the scope of this guide).

The identity element for addition is 0.
  Example: $7 + 0 = 7$ and $0 + 7 = 7$
  This is expressed algebraically as:
    $a + 0 = a$ and $0 + a = a$ in all cases, a is a real number

IMPORTANT NOTE: There is *no* identity element for subtraction.

The Commutative Property

Addition and multiplication are commutative. In this unit, students explore the commutative property of addition informally.

Commutative Property of Addition

This property states that the sum of the addends remains the same **regardless of the order in which they are added,** for all addends that are real numbers.

Example:
$$5 + 2 = 2 + 5$$
$$7 = 7$$
This is expressed algebraically as:
$a + b = b + a$ in all cases, a and b are real numbers

A concrete example of commutivity is the distance one travels, or "commutes," from home to school or work (H ➔ S) and then from school or work to home (S ➔ H), assuming, of course, the same route is used. (H ➔ S = S ➔ H)

Problem Types for Addition and Subtraction

In computation and story problems, students encounter three types of equations to solve. In each equation, two numbers are given as well as a computational symbol. What makes the problem types distinct is where the missing number or the unknown is situated in each equation. Three common problem types are: result unknown (complete the computation in an equation to get the solution); unknown situated after the computational sign and before the equal sign; and start of equation unknown.

These equation types can be written with any of the four computational operations and with any type of number. In this unit, however, students only encounter problems involving addition and subtraction with whole number as follows:

• *Result Unknown:* The most common problem type is one in which the unknown is determined by adding or subtracting two given numbers in an equation.

Addition Example

Alex had 5 cars. Chenoa gave him 4 more cars. How many cars does Alex have?

5 + 4 = ★

Subtraction Example

CJ had 7 tennis balls. He lost 3 balls at the park. How many tennis balls does CJ have?

7 − 3 = ★

In both of these story problems there is a clear starting number and a defined action followed by another defined number. The equation is straight forward to record, and the unknown is determined by simple computation. Number lines, counters, and fact families help students solve this type of problem.

• ***Unknown situated after the computational sign and before the equal sign:*** This is more difficult than the first type of problem because the unknown comes after the operation and before the result. However, since the start of the equation is known, there is a place to anchor the problem.

Addition Example

CJ had 9 sports awards in his room. He just received new awards from playing hockey. Now CJ has 12 awards altogether. How many new awards did CJ receive for playing hockey?

The starting point, 9, is clearly defined as the number of awards that CJ already has. Then he is given an unknown quantity, and finally, he has 12 altogether. The equation for this problem is 9 + ★ = 12.

Often, when students encounter this type of problem, they want to add the 9 and the 12 and record the answer as 21—especially when the word "altogether" is part of the problem. Even when posed as a computational problem without a story, seeing the symbol for addition, students think they need to add the two given numbers!

In this case, students need to understand how to read this equation and remember what equality means. Initially, it is beneficial to determine the unknown using manipulatives to build the problem

This is the problem type students solve in the first session of Activity 4. However, the computational operation is not given as part of the problem—students need to compare the two numbers and determine the operation. Solving this type of problem lays a foundation and prepares students for when they encounter this problem type.

with the information given or by comparing 9 and 12 on a number line. Later, as students gain fluency with fact families, they can use their knowledge of numbers to solve the equation.

Though it is also solvable by the inverse of addition (subtraction), the problem as stated is an addition problem with a missing addend.

Subtraction Example
Celia baked 12 cookies. She gave some away to her friends. She has 7 cookies left. How many cookies did Celia give away?

The start, 12 cookies, is clearly articulated and the action of taking away is also defined with 7 cookies remaining. The equation for this problem is $12 - \star = 7$.

Again, students need to understand how to read this equation and remember what equality means. Initially, it is beneficial to determine the unknown using manipulatives. Build the given numbers in the problem with concrete materials or by comparing 12 and 7 on a number line. Later, as students gain fluency with fact families, they can use their knowledge of numbers to solve the equation.

Though it is also solvable by the inverse of subtraction (addition), the problem as stated involves subtraction with a *missing subtrahend*.

• *Start of Equation Unknown.* This type of problem is most challenging to solve. There is no given starting point to hold onto or to anchor the problem. There is this nebulous unknown quantity to which another quantity is either added or subtracted, and then the result is given.

Addition Example
Alex had some marbles. Julia gave him 8 more marbles. Now he has 13 marbles. How many marbles did Alex have to start with?

There is an unknown quantity of marbles that Alex begins with. He adds 8 more to this unknown amount and ends up with 13 marbles. The equation for this problem is $\star + 8 = 13$.

Like the problem with the missing addend, students often want to add the 8 and 13 on first sight. It takes practice to read the equation and identify what the unknown represents.

To really understand what is being asked in the problem, the use of concrete materials supports student understanding. Build the given numbers, such as the 8 and 13, then review what each quantity represents and what is being asked. A comparison of the quantities and a reminder of equality will help students understand how to determine the missing addend. Here again, knowing fact families will support students with these problems.

Subtraction Example

Cindy had tickets to a hockey game. She gave 3 to her Uncle Ken. Cindy has 5 tickets left. How many tickets did she have to start with?

There is an unknown quantity of tickets that Cindy begins with. She gives away 3 from this unknown amount and is left with 5 tickets. The equation for this problem is $\star - 3 = 5$.

Again, the use of concrete materials supports student understanding. Build the given numbers, then review what each quantity represents and what the problem is asking. A comparison of the quantities and a reminder of equality will help students understand how to determine the missing minuend. Though this problem involves subtraction, the solution is greater than either of the two given numbers in the problem!

With practice and discussion of problems, students will become successful solvers of all problem types!

Learning and Acquiring Number Facts

Students acquire and retain number facts over time and by having the opportunity to go through stages of learning that build on one another. In the first stage, students construct a conceptual understanding of addition and subtraction, and learn how to record representations using numbers and symbols. Next, they work on fact families and develop strategies to compute. Then, they are able to solve symbolic representations of addition and subtraction problems, and finally, they commit the facts to memory. When students are asked to go directly to memorization, their ability to understand, retain, and use facts is fragile.

The child who is made dependent on her ability to memorize is painfully vulnerable.
—Robert Wirtz

The following three stages outline a developmental sequence designed to support students in learning and acquiring number facts.

• **Concrete Stage:** Before students even begin to add and subtract, they need as a prerequisite an understanding of number/quantity relationships. Building upon that, students develop the **conceptual understanding** of addition and subtraction by using **concrete materials**—such as counters, pictures, and fingers—in the context of stories and real world situations.

For example, using a "Hungry Shark" game (with blue paper and fish crackers or counters as the materials), students concretely add and subtract "fish" according to a story, as follows:

Teacher: *One day in the ocean 5 fish were swimming along.*
Students place 5 fish on their blue "ocean" papers.
Teacher: *Three more fish joined them. Add 3 more fish.*
Students add 3 more fish. They are concretely adding quantities.
Teacher: *How many fish are in the ocean now?*
Students count 8 fish altogether.
Teacher: *As the fish were swimming, along came a Hungry Shark. The shark loved to eat fish. When the fish saw the shark, they swam away, but the shark caught 2 fish and ate them both.*
Students play the role of the shark and eat or take 2 fish from the ocean. As the shark, students are concretely modeling subtraction!

The story continues with the students chiming in to provide opportunities to concretely add and subtract. Many other versions of this type of story can be used, including "Donut Monster" (using a baker, a donut monster, small oat cereal, and a donut tray) or "Shells on the Beach" (using shells, a seashore board, and a child collecting shells and giving some away).

In addition, single contextual problems can be modeled with concrete materials to help students develop an understanding of addition and subtraction. For example, students can find the solution to problems, such as the following two:

Kalynda had 7 special beads. She went to the store and bought 5 more. How many beads does Kalynda have altogether?

Michele has 9 toy elephants. She gives 2 of her elephants to her friend Kristen. How many toy elephants does she have left?

- **Connecting Stage:** After students have developed a conceptual understanding of addition and subtraction, they are ready to connect the symbolic notation to the concrete representations. They learn the meaning of the "+" and "−" and "=" symbols. As they build a representation of a story problem concretely, students learn how to record an equation that abstractly represents the concrete model. They can also use other mathematical tools, such as ten-frames and the number line, to solve and record equations.

While in this stage, students also work on individual numbers and generate number facts for them. For example, using the number 7, students can use counters in two colors to build the addition facts $(0 + 7, 1 + 6, 2 + 5, 3 + 4, 4 + 3, 5 + 2, 6 + 1, 7 + 0)$ and then record them as equations. As they build, the commutative property is informally introduced. By generating the facts, they have a concrete representation to connect to the equations for 7. Similarly, students can start with 7 objects and then subtract to generate the subtraction facts. Through these activities, students develop an understanding of the relationship between addition and subtraction facts. Strategies to solve problems are introduced (see the following section).

- **Abstract Stage:** During this stage, students have acquired fluency with number facts and are now able to solve addition and subtraction problems presented in symbolic form, such as $8 + 5 = \star$ or $13 - 6 = \S$ or any of the other problem types listed above. Strategies that depend on abstract knowledge are also developed and articulated (see the following section). In addition, students practice number facts for *short* amounts of time to support memorization. When practicing, a limited number of facts are studied to ensure that memorization occurs. Simultaneously, families support students in memorizing facts at home with guidance.

By going through these stages, students are anchored in the meaning of addition and subtraction, develop an understanding of the connections within fact families, acquire skills and strategies to solve computational problems, and can memorize facts with comprehension.

Addition and Subtraction Strategies for Single Digit Numbers

Here are some of the common strategies used for addition and subtraction, listed in order from most concrete to more abstract:

- **Direct Modeling:** Employ materials to build what the addition or subtraction problem is asking. Use counters, fingers, toys, or pencils—anything that allows a concrete representation to manipulate the quantities, according to the equation, to arrive at the solution.

- **"Add 0" Rule:** Early on, students build equations that have 0 as an addend and see that its addition has no effect on the sum. Generalize so that every time students see an equation that has a "number + 0" or "0 + number," the result is always the number being added to zero.

- **One More/One Less:** Make use of the order of numbers to go one forward to arrive at the solution to a "plus 1" problem, and count back one to arrive at the solution to a "minus 1" problem.

- **Count On/Count Back:** When using count on and count back strategies, fingers and number lines are often used as a tool.
  In addition, anchor the computation on the larger number and count on from that point. For example, in the equation $5 + 7 = \star$, students identify 7 as the larger number, and count on 5 beyond 7 to get to the sum of 12.
  In subtraction, start with the number given and count backwards the number that is being subtracted. For example, if the equation was $12 - 5 = \star$, start at the 12 and count back 5 numbers to get to the difference, 7.

- **Use Doubles (+1 or −1):** Be sure the double facts are practiced and memorized. Capitalize on those facts and extent them to doubles plus one as follows:
  $$7 + 8 = 7 + (7 + 1) = (7 + 7) + 1 = 14 + 1 = 15.$$
  Similarly, doubles minus one can be computed as follows:
  $$8 + 7 = 8 + (8 - 1) = (8 + 8) - 1 = 16 - 1 = 15.$$
  Once understood, these processes allow quick computation of consecutive numbers.

Many of these strategies make use of the Associative Property of Addition that states regardless of the order or groupings that three or more addends are summed, the sum will remain the same. The associative property of addition can be written as $(a + b) + c = a + (b + c)$.

• **"Hungry" Nines:** Ten is a "friendly" number to add to another number. Since 9 only needs 1 more to become a 10, whenever a 9 appears in an equation, it always wants to become a 10. (Nine is "hungry" to eat one more!) Rewrite an addend as a number plus 1. By adding the 1 to the 9, it becomes 10 and the addend is reduced by 1. The nine will become a ten as follows:

$6 + 9 = (5 + 1) + 9 = 5 + (1 + 9) = 5 + 10 = 15$ or
$3 + 9 + 4 = 3 + 9 + (1 + 3) = 3 + (9 + 1) + 3 = 3 + 10 + 3 = 10 + 6 = 16$.

• **Use 10 Facts:** Use the facts for sums of 10 to decompose or break apart the numbers in the problem. For example, given, $8 + 5$, use known fact $8 + 2 = 10$ to reconfigure the problem as follows: $8 + 5 = 8 + 2 + 3 = 10 + 3 = 13$. Similarly, in subtraction, break apart numbers to make use of 10 facts. For example, given $12 - 4$, first subtract 2 from 12 to get to 10, then subtract 2 more: $12 - 4 = 12 - (2 + 2) = (12 - 2) - 2 = 10 - 2 = 8$.

• **Derived Facts:** Make use of knowledge of facts and number sense to solve computation problems. Given $5 + 7 = •$, take advantage of doubles and an understanding of one more and one less. Take one from the seven and add it to the five, then it will be double sixes as follows: $5 + 7 = (5 + 1) + (7 - 1) = 6 + 6 = 12$.

A Word About Our Hero, ZERO!

Over 3,000 years ago, the Hindus in India were among the earliest people to use a symbol for zero. It was a dot or a little circle like an "o". They called it a *sunya* meaning "empty space."

Arabs learned about this symbol from the Hindus and called it a *zifr* or *sifr*. The Arabs took the Hindu number system to other lands including Europe, explaining why the numbers we write are called Hindu-Arabic numerals. The Latin word *zephirum*, based on the Hindu *sunya* and Arabic *zifr*, is probably where our word *zero* comes from.

There is also evidence that in other parts of the world, different cultures made use of zero. For example, in Madagascar, Africa, pebbles and a place value system were used to count soldiers. In Central America, the Maya people had a symbol for the quantity zero that looked like a shell.

How Did Algebra Get Its Name?

In the time of the Byzantine Empire lived a famous scholar named Mohammed ibn-Musa al-Khwarizmi. Al-Khwarizmi and his colleagues were scholars at the House of Wisdom, in Baghdad, and studied and wrote on algebra, geometry, and astronomy. The title of his treatise *Hisab al-jabr w'al-muqabala* in 825 C.E. gave us the word *"al-jabr"*—**algebra,** meaning "reduction" or "restoration"—and referred at that time to the process of removing negative terms from an equation. Over time, algebra came to refer to the study of equations. The term *"al-muqabala"* means **"balancing,"** the process of reducing positive terms of the same power when they occur on both sides of an equation.

In addition to his work in the area of algebra, al-Khwarizmi also wrote a book on arithmetic that became known in the 12th century by its Latin translation—*Algoritmi de numero Indorum.* (The word **algorithm,** meaning a rule for computation, is derived from *"algoritmi,"* the Latin form of al-Khwarizmi's name.) This book introduced Western Europe to Hindu-Arabic numerals and computations that use them—which is our arithmetic today! (Interestingly, in the 15th and 16th centuries, the Italians distinguished algebra from arithmetic by calling algebra the *greater art* and arithmetic the *lesser art.*)

In Spain, the Moors introduced a more common meaning of the Arabic term *"al-jabr."* The word *"algebrista"* evolved to mean a person who re-set, or "restored," broken bones. The word found its way to Italy in the 16th century, and in Europe the word "algebra" expanded to mean the art of bone setting.

In the 18th century, Swiss mathematician Leonhard Euler's book, *Instructions in Algebra,* became the model of algebra texts and firmly established the name for both Arabic and European scholars. (He also popularized the symbol for pi, invented by English mathematician William Jones.) You may want to encourage your students to do some research on the story of algebra, as it affirms the rich tapestry of multicultural and multinational contributions to mathematics and science. There were many other world mathematical influences that went into creating what we call algebra today! ■

Teacher's Outline

ACTIVITY 1: INTRODUCING ZERO

Session 1: What We Know and Wonder about Zero

■ Getting Ready
1. Prepare first two class charts; have blank chart paper on hand.
2. Read **Letter to Families.** Duplicate it or your own version.
3. Gather markers, tape, pre-made charts, and extra chart paper.

■ Zero the Hero
1. Write "zero" on board. Have students read it and share with neighbor what they know about zero.
2. Post "Our Ideas about Zero" chart. Ask class to share ideas.
3. Record students' ideas and encourage explanations. Check that class agrees with statements about zero. Even if there is disagreement, record the idea, but mark it.
4. Ask what students wonder or would like to find out about zero.
5. Post "What We Wonder about Zero" chart and record responses.
6. Say this new math unit will feature zero.
7. For homework, have students talk to families about zero. Distribute letters to students.

Session 2: Zero, One, Two, Three: What Number Will It Be?

■ Getting Ready
1. Make dice for game—one die for each student pair.
2. Decide which version of data sheet to use. Copy one for each student pair.
3. Make or purchase a mathematics journal for each student.
4. Prepare a "What We Learned" and a "Further Investigations" chart.
5. Familiarize yourself with "Chapter 1: Zero Becomes Something" story.
6. Gather dice, data sheets, markers, tape, and charts.

■ Introducing the Game
1. Review students' ideas about zero. Ask for their families' ideas.
2. As students respond, modify charts made in Session 1.
3. Say you have a game for students to play. Show the data sheet. Have them read the title.
4. Say game is played with special die with numbers 0, 1, 2, and 3. Don't emphasize that zero is on three faces.
5. Explain that in the game, partners take turns rolling die. Numbers rolled are used to make a two- or three-digit number (depending on data sheet selected).
6. Show data sheet again and review names of place value (tens and ones or hundreds, tens, and ones) for numbers students will make.
7. With a student partner, demonstrate how to use data sheet and play game.

■ Playing the Game

1. Distribute data sheet and die to each pair. Let the games begin!
2. Circulate and assist as necessary.
3. When all have filled in all digits for five numbers and identified the highest, ask questions to help them analyze how they used zero.
4. At end of discussion, ask what students learned about zero. Have them talk to their partners before they respond to the class.
5. Post two new charts and record their suggestions. Record inaccurate ideas or those you are unsure about on "Further Investigations" chart.
6. Distribute journals. Have students label them as "mathematics journal" and put their names on them. Provide time for students to record what they learned about zero in journals.
7. Collect journals to assess student thinking.
8. Read aloud the story. As you do so, write key words, ideas, or numbers on the board. Actively involve students, and encourage comments and discussion.

ACTIVITY 2: COMPARING NUMBERS

Session 1: Into the Trash It Goes!

■ Getting Ready

1. Decide which version of data sheet to use. Copy one per student and several extra sheets.
2. Make two copies of the appropriate place value board for each pair of students.
3. Gather the base 10 material.
4. Have bags of base 10 material, dice, place value boards, and data sheets ready to distribute.
5. Familiarize yourself with "Chapter 2: Zero's Family" story.
6. Have markers available to add to "What We Learned" chart.

■ Sum of Two Standard Dice

1. Review "What We Learned" chart. Check for understanding and agreement.
2. Say you have a new game for students to play in which they will make numbers by rolling standard dice.
3. Ask questions to see what students know about standard dice.
4. Show a pair of standard dice. Have students talk to a partner about what numbers can be made with two standard dice.
5. Have students share their ideas and write on board the possible sums (2 through 12) and ways you can get them. Make sure they understand the number 1 cannot be obtained when using sum of two standard dice.
6. Say they'll use these dice to play "Into the Trash It Goes!" game.

■ Introducing the Game

1. Show data sheet. Have students identify place values (tens and ones or hundreds, tens, and ones) of the number they'll build.
2. Say they'll use the sum of the dice to fill in digits on their sheets. Ask if any sums rolled will be difficult to record.
3. Explain that when sum of roll is 10, 11, or 12, they record a 0. Review the numbers that can be recorded on sheets.
4. Say for now object is to make the highest number possible. Later they'll play game again and try for lowest number.
5. Point out "trash can." Explain that one of the sums they roll can be "thrown" into the trash.
6. With a student partner, demonstrate how to play game and record on data sheet.
7. Demonstrate how players will build their numbers using base 10 materials, and how to decompose numbers into their place value parts (as on bottom of data sheet).

■ Partners Play the Game

1. Review how to play. For first two games, make highest number possible, circling the word HIGHEST on data sheet.
2. Distribute dice, place value boards, data sheets, base ten material. As students play, circulate to assist.
3. When most have played two games, focus class for a discussion. Pose questions as in guide.
4. Call on students and record their numbers on the board. Determine largest. Order numbers from highest to lowest.
5. Ask questions, as in guide, to focus thinking and discussion of what they did when they "rolled" a zero.
6. Ask for then record strategies for making largest number possible.
7. Provide time for partners to play game again with the object of making the lowest number possible. Remind them to circle the word LOWEST on data sheet.
8. If students complete all their data sheets, encourage them to continue playing and record their numbers in their journals.
9. As students finish, record new ideas on "What We Learned" chart. Record questions on "Further Investigations" chart.
10. Pose problem as in guide for students to respond to in their journals. After an appropriate amount of writing time, collect journals.
11. Read aloud the story. As you do so, write key words, ideas, or numbers on the board. Actively involve students, and encourage comments and discussion.
12. Continue to provide opportunities for students to play the game. If they record them in their journals, be sure they write highest or lowest on the page. Discuss the differences that creates in the game and encourage them to record their ideas in their journals.

Session 2: Greater Than, Less Than, or Equal To?

■ Getting Ready

1. Have the dice, base 10 materials, and place value boards from first session ready to distribute.
2. Have journals ready.

■ Rollin' and Recordin'

1. Tell students they will play another game using a 0–3 die and a standard 1–6 die. Demonstrate on board as detailed in the guide.
2. Introduce or review symbols for: greater than (>), less than (<), and equal to (=). Add the appropriate symbol to the numbers created in the demonstration.
3. Tell students they'll work with a partner to make two two- or three-digit numbers, record the numbers in journals, then compare the numbers and record the correct symbol between them.
4. Demonstrate, with the example in guide, how to play the game with a partner and record it in the journal.

■ Partners Play Independently

1. Review procedure. Remind students to record starting with one's place.
2. Pair students, and distribute dice and base 10 materials.
3. As students play, circulate and check that they build numbers with base 10 materials and use the symbolic notation accurately.
4. When students finish, record symbolic notation and definitions on "What We Learned" chart. Include an example of each.
5. Have students record symbols and definitions in journals.

ACTIVITY 3: MOVING ON THE NUMBER LINE

Session 1: The Answer Is Zero

■ Getting Ready

1. Decide how to obtain or make number lines.
2. Decide what small plastic animal or marker students will use to move along number line. Gather one for each student.
3. Familiarize yourself with "Chapter 3: Zero's Home" story.
4. Have journals available for students to record number sentences derived from frog stories.

■ Home Sweet Home

1. Distribute a number line to each student. Have them locate various numbers on it.

2. Say a frog lives at 0 on the number line. It hops to other numbers, but always returns home to 0. They'll help the frog get home.

3. Give a frog to each student, and have them put it on the 0.

4. Start with a story as in guide.

5. Continue with other stories to help students become familiar with the number line. Be sure stories have frog moving in both positive and negative directions.

■ Recording Froggie's Movements

1. Tell students you want to record the frog's movements with numbers and symbols, not words.

2. As you tell another story, record the number sentences on the board. Follow example as in guide.

■ More Hopping Around!

1. Tell similar stories and have students move frogs along number line. Continue to record number sentences and have students record them in their journals.

2. Encourage students to tell stories about frog's movements.

3. Ask what students learned from using the number line and record on "What We Learned" chart. Add symbols for writing equations along with definitions.

4. Students may notice that zero plus a number equals that number and/or any number minus itself always equals zero. Add these to chart.

5. Have students record in their journals the new information added to chart.

6. Read aloud the story. As you do so, write key words, ideas, or numbers on the board. Actively involve students, and encourage comments and discussion.

7. For homework, have students record a series of equations to represent one adventure of Froggie along the number line. Remind them to have Froggie begin and end at 0.

Session 2: 1's the One!

■ Getting Ready

1. Gather number lines and small plastic animals (or markers) used in Session 1.

2. Have journals available for students to record number sentences from frog stories.

■ 1 is THE One!

1. Distribute number lines and small animals. Have several students share the series of equation they did for homework.

2. Say Froggie has moved to a new home at number 1. Have students find 1 on the number line. Froggie likes to move from the 1, but always returns there at the end of her moves.

3. Record a 1 on board. Have students place their frogs on the number 1.

4. Begin a new story, as in guide. Have students record equations for story in journals.

5. Continue to give similar problems and have students record the equations.
6. Have pairs of students make up a story and record the equations. As they work, circulate and ask questions to check for understanding.
7. See if students want to add to "What We Learned" chart. If you add to chart, have students record new information in their journals.

Session 3: Algebra in Action

■ Getting Ready
1. Gather number lines and small plastic animals or markers used in previous sessions.
2. Have journals available for students to record number sentences.

■ Solving Equations Using the Number Line
1. When students understand how to use equations to represent frog's movements, provide a challenge.
2. Say the frog may begin on any number and end at any different number.
3. Begin with an equation that has a starting and ending point. Students determine how many hops frog needs to move forward or backward to solve the equation.
4. Use an example, as in guide, to introduce and encourage discussion of the meaning of equality.

■ This Is Algebra!
1. Tell students they solved an equation. A number and operation were needed to make the equation complete. When students figured out the missing information, they solved the equation.
2. When students find the missing number in the equation they are doing algebra! Ask if anyone has heard of algebra and listen to what they know.
3. Provide another equation with a missing number. Have students read equation aloud. Explain that the blank represents a missing number—called an unknown (or variable). It can also be shown as a symbol, such as a star or letter.
4. Show how to use a symbol for the variable.
5. Have students solve the equation using number lines. Substitute in the answer to see if the equation is true.
6. Provide another equation for students to solve with a partner. Have them record equation in journals and use frogs and number lines to solve it.
7. Have students explain the solution. Check that students record all steps of the solution including the equality.
8. Provide additional problems. Circulate and assist as needed.
9. Ask if they want to add to the "What We Learned" chart. If you add new information, have students record it in their journals.

ACTIVITY 4: SOLVING EQUATIONS

Session 1: What's Missing?

■ Getting Ready
1. Copy one mini-book for each student and at least four more copies.
2. Practice making mini-book before demonstrating to students. You'll need two pre-made books to model the game.
3. Decide which dice your students will use.
4. Have copies of mini-book templates and scissors ready to demonstrate how to make books. Also have available pre-made books and journals.
5. Have dice ready to distribute and number lines available (counters are optional).
6. Familiarize yourself with "Chapter 4: Number Tricks" story.

■ Making the Mini-Book
1. Show students pre-made book. Say they'll make one like it to record equations and write stories to go with equations.
2. Distribute scissors and mini-book templates. Have students do each step in making the book after you demonstrate what to do.
3. Congratulate students on having made a book, then have them write their names on covers.

■ Rolling and Recording
1. Gather students and show how to fill their books. Have dice, pre-made books, and number lines ready.
2. Select a student partner. Each of you writes name on cover of a pre-made book.
3. Open book and go over first page with students. Be sure they note location of "roll #1" and "roll #2" boxes and star.
4. Demonstrate how to roll dice and record in book, as in guide.

■ Solving
1. Walk students through how to solve equation in your book then partner's book.
2. Point out the other page ("My Story Problem"). Say they'll complete that after making equations.

■ Recording and Solving Equations
1. Have partners work together to complete three equations in their books. Mention that number lines are available.
2. Circulate and assist. If some pairs finish quickly, have them make another book and generate more equations.

■ Writing Story Problems
1. When students have completed equations, begin discussion on how to write story problems.
2. Go back to equation, "9 − 4 = 5." Ask partners to tell each other a story for this equation.

3. Listen to a few stories. Identify action words. Brainstorm words used in story problems. Record them on "What We Learned" chart.
4. Tell stories for both addition and subtraction and generate words for both types of story problems (see likely list in guide).
5. Have students record words in journals.
6. Make sure students realize there's no separate "My Story Problem" page for third equation; they'll write that story problem in journals.
7. Have students write stories for their equations.
8. Read aloud the story. As you do so, write key words, ideas, or numbers on the board. Actively involve students, and encourage comments and discussion.

Session 2: More Equations to Solve

■ Getting Ready
1. Based upon students' skills and abilities, vary problem types and level of difficulty.
2. Read about different problem types in guide. Choose either a Result Unknown or Start Unknown problem type. Decide on the operation (addition or subtraction) to be used and write it in each equation.
3. Make one copy per student of the appropriate mini-book template. Make an extra if students need guidance on making the book. Also make two pre-made books.
4. Decide which dice students will use.
5. Gather scissors, dice, pre-made books, and number lines.
6. Familiarize yourself with "Chapter 5: One Last Trick Featuring Zero" story.

■ Making and Using New Books
1. Distribute scissors and new version of mini-book. Have students make a new book, then compare it to the original one.
2. Guide students to location of unknown in new book.
3. Select a partner to demonstrate how to complete the equations in the book.
4. Ask how to solve for the unknown in the equations. Record the appropriate number in the star in each book.
5. Organize students into pairs, distribute dice, then have students generate and solve equations.
6. After students have completed three equations in their books, have them write story problems for each, reminding them the story for the third equation will be put in journals.
7. Read aloud the story. As you do so, write key words, ideas, or numbers on the board. Actively involve students, and encourage comments and discussion.

ASSESSMENT SUGGESTIONS

These outcomes address the NCTM Algebra and Number and Operations standards explained on pages 4–5. Though the outcomes do not specifically use the word "algebra," the outcomes spell out the content that is taught in the classroom and meets the standards for grades one and two. For example, the Algebra standard that states, "students represent and analyze mathematical situations using algebraic symbols" is embedded in Outcomes 2, 3, 4, 5, and 6.

Anticipated Student Outcomes

1. Students deepen their **understanding of the number zero** and its **role in the base 10 system.**

2. Students **select appropriate symbols,** including greater than (>), less than (<), and equal to (=) for numeric relationships to make an expression or equation true.

3. Students deepen their understanding of the **meaning of addition** and **subtraction** and the symbols "+" and "−".

4. Students are able to **write number sentences** (equations) and **solve problems** for situations involving addition and subtraction. They can also **create problem situations** to accompany equations.

5. Students are able to **use symbols to represent unknowns** (called variables in algebra) in addition and subtraction equations. Students demonstrate increased ability to **solve an equation** that has an unknown.

6. Students develop an understanding of the following **properties of Numbers and Operations:**

   • Identity Element of Addition
   • Commutative Property of Addition

Embedded Assessment Activities

As you teach and facilitate the activities in this guide, you may need to adjust the content to fit the skills and abilities of your students. This may mean taking a step backward, or adjusting the numbers students work with, or providing more challenging problems. As the teacher, you are constantly assessing as you implement the curriculum. Throughout the unit, there are embedded assessments that you will find in each activity as well as ones that are specific to each activity.

Classroom Discourse. Throughout the unit, you serve as a facilitator helping students to articulate their thinking and to build on each other's thinking as well as listen to one another. Student questions also provide opportunities for classmates to demonstrate their knowledge by answer-

Ideas ◄

Suggestions ◄

Resources ◄

that lead to Great Explorations
in Math and Science!

Get Connected!

www.lhsgems.o

01 LAWRENCE HALL OF SCIENCE # 5200

61571-25775-62-X

BUSINESS REPLY MAIL
FIRST-CLASS MAIL   PERMIT NO 7   BERKELEY CA

POSTAGE WILL BE PAID BY ADDRESSEE

UNIVERSITY OF CALIFORNIA BERKELEY
GEMS
LAWRENCE HALL OF SCIENCE
PO BOX 16000
BERKELEY CA 94701-9700

ing questions. Class discussions provide valuable insights into students' understanding of the content. As their guide, you can ask clarifying questions or provide additional information to help students gain understanding.

Classroom Charts. Throughout the unit, students contribute to class charts. After each session, the "What We Learned" chart provides a forum for solidifying the concepts and skills that were covered—including definitions, symbols, examples, etc. It also becomes the shared "class knowledge" that can be accessed and referred to in discussions. The "Further Investigations" chart provides a window on students' questions, misconceptions, and additional knowledge about content. Both inform you about how well students are grasping the content and help you adjust the pacing accordingly.

Student Journals. The students' journals provide a record of their class work and their learning throughout the unit. At the end of most activities, there is a prompt that gets at the heart of the day's learning. The students' responses in their journals inform you about each student's individual progress and understanding. By reading through all the journals, you can have a snapshot of the understanding of the class as a whole. This can help you make strategic decisions about pacing.

There are also specific, built-in assessments in each activity, including the following strategic assessments and the anticipated outcomes they address.

Our Ideas About Zero. (Activity 1, Session 1) In this first activity in the unit, students are asked what they know about zero. Their responses provide a pre-assessment of their understanding about zero. (Addresses outcome 1)

Playing the Game Debrief. (Activity 1, Session 2) Class discussion about how students used the number zero in the "Zero, One, Two, Three…" game. (Outcome 1)

Presto Change-O Game. (Activity 2, Going Further) Students build numbers with place value materials. (Outcomes 1 and 2)

Guess My Number. (Activity 2, Going Further) Students guess a number based on clues related to the digit values in the number. (Outcomes 1 and 2)

Frog Moves on the Number Line. (Activity 3, Session 1) For homework, students record a series of equations that represents the movements of the frog along a number line. (Outcomes 1, 2, 3, 4)

Writing Story Problems. (Activity 4, Session 1) Students create story problems with an unknown. (Outcomes 2, 3, 4, 5, 6)

Journal Prompt. (Going Further for the Whole Unit) Students are asked why zero is a hero and what is special about zero. (Outcomes 1 and 6)

Additional Assessment Ideas

Please see the two special assessments for this unit:

Creating and Comparing Numbers on pages 111–113. (Outcomes 1, 2, 3)

Writing and Solving Equations on pages 114–115. (Outcomes 4, 5, 6)

High and Low Number Games

You are playing a game with your friend.
You have rolled three numbers: **0, 7, 4**

1. If the HIGHEST number wins, what number would you make with **0, 7, 4** ?

Highest Number: _____

How do you know this is the highest number?

_____

_____

_____

2. If the LOWEST number wins, what number would you make with **0, 7, 4** ?

Lowest Number: _____

How do you know this is the lowest number?

_____

_____

_____

3. Use the **0, 7, 4** to make a number that is BETWEEN the highest and lowest numbers.

Number BETWEEN the highest and lowest: _____

How do you know it is BETWEEN?

_____

_____

_____

Great Than? Less Than? or Equal To?

Ben and Maria are playing the Into the Trash It Goes! game. Here is the start of the game:

Player 1: Ben

6 __ __ [1] Trash

Player 2: Maria

__ 6 __ [2] Trash

1. At the end of the game, Ben's number is equal to Maria's number. They rolled a _____ and a _____. Fill in their numbers.

Player 1: Ben

6 __ __ [1] Trash

=

Player 2: Maria

__ 6 __ [2] Trash

2. Now, Ben's number is GREATER than Maria's number. This time they rolled a _____ and a _____. Fill in their numbers.

Player 1: Ben

6 __ __ [1] Trash

>

Player 2: Maria

__ 6 __ [2] Trash

3. Now, Ben's number is LESS than Maria's number. This time they rolled a _____ and a _____. Fill in their numbers.

Player 1: Ben

6 __ __ [1] Trash

<

Player 2: Maria

__ 6 __ [2] Trash

4. Here is the last game they played.
   Maria's number is GREATER than Ben's number.
   Ben rolled a 1, 5, 4, 1 and Maria rolled a 1, 3, 7, 2.
   Fill in their numbers. Don't forget to fill the trash!

Player 1: Ben   Player 2: Maria

   — — — Trash   <   — — — Trash

5. Look at the two numbers. Compare the numbers.
   Write the symbol between the numbers to show how they compare.

= (equal to)   > (greater than)   < (less than)

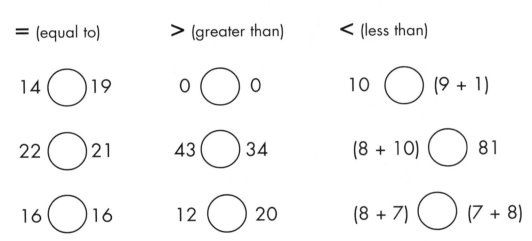

14 ◯ 19   0 ◯ 0   10 ◯ (9 + 1)

22 ◯ 21   43 ◯ 34   (8 + 10) ◯ 81

16 ◯ 16   12 ◯ 20   (8 + 7) ◯ (7 + 8)

Writing and Solving Equations

1. Alice had 7 pencils. Her dad gave her 5 more pencils.
   Alice wants to know how many pencils she has now.
   Help Alice. How many pencils does Alice have now?

   Write an equation and find the answer.   Show your work!

2. Colin has 14 trucks. He gives 3 trucks to Miguel.
   They want to know how many trucks Colin has left.
   Help them. How many trucks does Colin have now?

   Write an equation and find the answer.   Show your work!

3. José has 7 cousins. Laura has 11 cousins.

   Who has more cousins?_____

   How many more cousins does Laura have than José?_____

   Write an equation for this problem:

4. Tara and DeShawn like to collect shells. Today they found
   14 shells altogether. DeShawn found 6 of the shells.
   They want to know how many shells Tara picked up.
   How many did Tara find?

   Write an equation and find the answer.   Show your work!

Solve these equations:

⬡ + 7 = 11   15 − △ = 8

12 − 3 = ☆   9 + ▢ = 14

Write in the correct sign + or − in these equations:

7 ◯ 3 = 10   13 ◯ 5 = 8

14 ◯ 7 = 7   8 ◯ 9 = 17

Fill in two numbers that will make this equation equal:

____ + ____ = 16

Write a story that goes with the equation:

RESOURCES & LITERATURE CONNECTIONS

Sources

Classroom-Ready Materials Kits

Carolina Biological Supply® is the exclusive distributor of fully prepared GEMS Kits®, which contain all the materials you need for full classroom presentation of GEMS units. For more information, please visit www.carolina.com/GEMS or call (800) 227-1150.

Base Ten Material

The Math Learning Center
P.O. Box 3226
Salem, OR 97302
(800) 575-8130
www.mlc.pdx.edu

Educators Outlet
P.O. Box 397
Timnath, CO 80547
(800) 315-2212
www.educatorsoutlet.com

Number Line

Educators Outlet
see address above

Icosahedron Dice

Math 'n' Stuff
8926 Roosevelt Way NE
Seattle, WA 98115
(206) 522-8891
fax (206) 522-1235
www.mathnificent.com

Small Plastic Frogs

Primary Concepts
Box 10043
Berkeley, CA 94709
(800) 660-8646
www.primaryconcepts.com

Related Curriculum Material

Family Math for Young Children
Comparing
by Grace Davila Coates and Jean Kerr Stenmark
EQUALS/Lawrence Hall of Science, Berkeley, CA
(1997; 196 pp.)

Designed for families to explore mathematics with young children in engaging, and concrete ways. The activities on Mixtures particularly connect to the algebraic thinking activities in this unit.

Groundworks: Algebraic Thinking
by Carole Greenes and Carol Findell
Creative Publications
Wright Group/McGraw-Hill, Bothell, WA

The Groundworks series allows teachers to begin laying the foundation for algebraic thinking in first grade and continues through seventh. The reproducible books are organized around six big ideas of algebra: representation, balance, variable, function, proportional reasoning, and inductive reasoning. The books in the Algebraic Thinking category are for students in grades 1–3. Each grade level has a 128-page teacher resource book and a 32-

page student workbook. These books are a great resource to follow this GEMS unit and provide additional practice in algebraic thinking and problem solving.

Nonfiction for the Teacher

Algebra for Dummies
by Mary Jane Sterling
Hungry Minds/Wiley, New York, NY
(2001; 384 pp.)

This book covers everything from fractions to quadratic equations. Includes real-world examples and story problems. And of course, there are no "dummies" in mathematics, just people who think they are because they were not taught in creative and effective ways!

Algebra to Go
A Mathematics Handbook
by the Great Source Education Group Staff
Great Source Education Group/Houghton Mifflin,
Boston, MA
(2000; 523 pp.)

Presents key and often complex math topics in ways
that are clear and easily understandable—from numera-
tion and number theory to estimation and linear and
non-linear equations. Provides detailed explanations,
accessible charts and graphs, and examples to help
understand and retain algebraic concepts.

Algebraic Thinking, Grades K–12
Readings from NCTM's School-Based Journals and Other Publications
edited by Barbara Moses
National Council of Teachers of Mathematics, Reston, VA
(1999; 392 pp.)

Helps teachers understand the development of algebraic
thinking and the types of activities at different grade
levels that can foster such thinking in children. Includes
a comprehensive collection of 59 specially selected
articles from various NCTM publications and pub-
lished work from other organizations.

Math to Know
A Mathematics Handbook
by Mary C. Cavanagh
Great Source Education Group/Houghton Mifflin,
Boston, MA
(2000; 483 pp.)

This comprehensive resource provides clear explanations and numerous examples to understand important
math concepts including basic operations, mental math
and estimation, fractions and decimals, algebra, geometry, graphing, statistics and probability. Contains an
especially helpful chapter on algebraic thinking.

Navigating through Algebra in Prekindergarten–Grade 2
by Carole Greenes, Mary Cavanagh, Linda Dacey, Carol
Findell, and Mariam Small
National Council of Teachers of Mathematics, Reston, VA
(2001; 90 pp.)

The Navigation series is designed to provide ideas and
activities to support the implementation of *Principles
and Standards for School Mathematics*. Activities introduce
and promote familiarity with patterns, variables and
equality, and relations and functions. Features margin
notes with teaching tips, anticipated student responses,
assessment ideas, and references to some of the resources on the CD-ROM included with the book.

Principles and Standards for School Mathematics
National Council of Teachers of Mathematics, Reston, VA
(2000; 402 pp.)

Intended as a resource and guide for educators and
administrators of students in grades prekindergarten
though 12. Includes a set of six principles to guide the
character of mathematics programs and 10 content and
process standards for students to achieve throughout
their math education. Standards are divided into grade
level groupings as follows: Prekindergarten–2, Grades
3–5, Grades 6–8, and Grades 9–12.

Radical Equations
Math Literacy and Civil Rights
by Robert P. Moses and Charles E. Cobb, Jr.
Beacon Press, Boston, MA
(2001; 256 pp.)

Bob Moses's work to organize black voters in Mississippi famously transformed the political power of entire
communities. Nearly 40 years later, Moses is organizing
again, this time as teacher and founder of the national
math literacy program called the Algebra Project. Moses
suggests that the crisis in math literacy in poor communities is as urgent as the crisis of political access in
Mississippi in 1961. See also Internet section for more
information on the Algebra Project.

A Survey of Mathematics:
Elementary Concepts and Their Historical Development
by Vivian Shaw Groza
(1968; out of print)

Although this book is out of print, it can be purchased online. An excellent user-friendly resource book for teachers to read and understand math concepts. Contains useful historical and background information on mathematics.

Magazines

Algebraic Thinking Focus Issue, *Teaching Children Mathematics,* February 1997, Vol. 3, No. 6.

"Children's Understanding of Equality: A Foundation for Algebra," *Teaching Children Mathematics,* December 1999, Vol. 5, No. 4, pp. 232–236.

"Developing Algebraic Reasoning in the Elementary Grades," *Teaching Children Mathematics,* December 1998, Vol. 4, No. 4, pp. 225–229.

"Developing Elementary Teachers' Algebra Eyes and Ears," *Teaching Children Mathematics,* October 2003, Vol. 10, No. 2, pp. 70–77.

"Meaningful Mathematical Representations and Early Algebraic Reasoning," *Teaching Children Mathematics,* October 2002, Vol. 9, No. 2, pp. 76–80.

"The Struggle to Link Written Symbols with Understandings: An Update," *Arithmetic Teacher,* March 1989, Vol. 36, pp. 38–44.

Research Brief

"Algebra in the Elementary Grades," *in Brief,* Fall 2000, Vol. 1, No. 2.
> *in Brief* is a publication of the National Center for Improving Student Learning and Achievement in Mathematics and Science, at the Wisconsin Center for Education Research, University of Wisconsin-Madison. It is available free upon request or it can be downloaded as a pdf file at www.wcer.wisc.edu/ncisla/publications/briefs/fall2000.pdf

Nonfiction for Students

G is for Googol
A Math Alphabet Book
by David M. Schwartz;
illustrated by Marissa Moss
Tricycle Press, Berkeley, CA
(1998; 57 pp.)

Explains the meaning of mathematical terms which begin with the letters of the alphabet from abacus to a zillion. The meaning of "Googol" (the number 1 followed by 100 zeros) is particularly apt for this unit.

The Grapes of Math
Mind Stretching Math Riddles
by Greg Tang;
illustrated by Harry Briggs
Scholastic, New York, NY
(2001; 40 pp.)

This innovative book challenges children—and parents—to open their minds and solve problems in new and unexpected ways. By looking for patterns, symmetries, and familiar number combinations displayed with eye-catching pictures, math skills and young minds grow.

Math Talk
Mathematical Ideas in Poems for Two Voices
by Theoni Pappas
Wide World Publishing/Tetra, San Carlos, CA
(1991; 72 pp.)

Presents mathematical ideas through poetic dialogues designed to be read by two people. The forward in the book states "Mathematical ideas can be learned through art, reading, conversations, lectures. Therefore, why not link mathematical ideas and poetic dialogues?" Of particular relevance to this unit are the poems about numbers and operations, and they could be read chorally by a class.

Zero is Not Nothing
by Mindel and Harry Sitomer;
illustrated by Richard Cuffari
Thomas Y. Crowell, New York, NY
(1978; 32 pp.)

This lively and engaging book about zero provides practical everyday examples of the mathematical meaning of zero. From its importance as a place holder to it being the start of any measurement, this book is a compliment to the concepts in the unit. Even though written in 1978, the illustrations and content are timeless and the historical background is a bonus!

Zero
Is it Something? Is it Nothing?
by Claudia Zaslavsky;
illustrated by Jeni Bassett
Franklin Watts, New York, NY
(1989; 32 pp.)

This book illustrates the concept of zero as a number that can represent nothing at all or serve as a place holder in a multi-digit number—something very important! Zero is also compared to an "o" and there are practical examples of its uses. Zero—as the identity element for addition—is illustrated, and the book ends with riddles about zero. Illustrations are cartoon-like and geared toward a young audience.

Fiction for Students

12 Ways to Get to 11
by Eve Merriam;
illustrated by Bernie Karlin
Simon & Schuster, New York, NY
(1993; 32 pp.)
Grades K–2

Objects that add up to 11 are clearly illustrated on two-page spreads. One illustration includes three sets of triplets and a pair of twins in strollers, while another features a pond with frogs, turtles, and dragonflies. Each illustration is a great tool for representing the quantity of 11 as well as for generating equations for 11.

Among the Odds & Evens
A Tale of Adventure
by Priscilla Turner;
illustrated by Whitney Turner
Farrar Straus Giroux, New York, NY
(1999; 32 pp.)
Grades 2–4

When X and Y crash in the land of Wontoo, they cannot understand how the Numbers live the way they do, until they not only get used to it, but decide they want to stay in Wontoo. Introduces odd and even concepts, some of which may be beyond your students understanding.

Dinosaur Deals
by Stuart J. Murphy;
illustrated by Kevin O'Malley
HarperCollins, New York, NY
(2001; 30 pp.)
Grades 2–3

Using dinosaur trading cards as a theme, the concept of equivalent values is explored. Mike and his brother, Andy, go to a trading fair in hopes of finding a *Tyrannosaurus rex* card. By making various trades they are successful in getting the coveted item. The story contains just the right amount of tension as well as tidbits of dinosaur facts interspersed among the math concepts. A concluding page gives suggestions for various math activities that correlate with this MathStart book.

Earth Day—Hooray!

by Stuart J. Murphy;
illustrated by Renee Andriani
HarperCollins, New York, NY
(2004; 40 pp.)
Grades 2–3

After the Maple Street School Save-the-Planet Club cleans up the local park for Earth Day, the park still needs some beautifying. The club decides to recycle aluminum cans to raise money for flowers. The text follows their efforts at collecting the cans and bagging them into groups of 10, 100, and 1,000. As the club posts their totals in the school hallway, readers see the bags and the way the numbers add up to make a grand total. Flyers, posters, and even the teacher's blackboard feature facts about recycling and the beginnings of Earth Day. Wonderful tie-in to the place value activities in the guide. A MathStart book.

Even Steven and Odd Todd

by Kathryn Cristaldi;
illustrated by Henry B. Morehouse
Scholastic, New York, NY
(1996; 32 pp.)
Grades 1–3

The arrival of Cousin Odd Todd greatly upsets Even Steven who likes everything to come in even numbers. Through their differing number preferences, the concept of even and odd is presented in an enjoyable and understandable context. Includes activities and games. From the Hello Reader! Math Series.

How Many Snails?
A Counting Book

by Paul Giganti, Jr.;
illustrated by Donald Crews
William Morrow, New York, NY
(1988; 32 pp.)
Grades K–3

As a young child takes walks to different places, he or she wonders about the numbers of the things seen. The book poses questions that invite the child to look at attributes and count sets of objects in a variety of ways. The story can be used to generate equations and inequalities.

Mission: Addition

by Loreen Leedy
Scholastic, New York, NY
(1997; 32 pp.)
Grades 1–2

A great book to reinforce the basics of addition including symbols, commutative property, and multiple addends. Engaging problems are posed with illustrations to accompany them. Readers also find some arithmetic errors to correct!

My Little Sister Ate One Hare

by Bill Grossman;
illustrated by Kevin Hawkes
Crown Publishers, New York, NY
(1996; 24 pp.)
Grades K–3

A delightfully "yucky" counting book that ends with a new twist. After the little sister eats creatures in quantities from one to nine, 10 healthy peas put her over the edge. Have students find out how many animals little sister ate!

Safari Park

by Stuart J. Murphy;
illustrated by Steve Bjorkman
HarperCollins, New York, NY
(2002; 40 pp.)
Grades 2–3

Grandpa has taken his five grandchildren to Safari Park and given each of them 20 tickets. As each of the kids goes on a ride, there is an illustration of how many tickets have been used up and a question mark for the number of tickets remaining to equal the original 20. The concept of finding an unknown ties in directly with the activities in this unit. From the MathStart series.

Sea Sums

by Joy N. Hulme;
illustrated by Carol Schwartz
Hyperion Books, New York, NY
(1996; 32 pp.)
Grades K–2

As the sea creatures living near a coral reef swim in and out of the area, readers are introduced to counting, addition, and subtraction. Written in poetry form and illustrated with beautiful gouache paintings.

Shark Swimathon
by Stuart J. Murphy;
illustrated by Lynne Cravath
HarperCollins, New York, NY
(2001; 32 pp.)
Grades 2–3

As members of a shark swim team do laps to qualify for swim camp, readers can practice subtracting two-digit numbers to see how many laps are left to go. Illustrations explain regrouping and recording techniques. Activities are included at the end of this MathStart book.

Ten Friends
by Bruce Goldstone;
illustrated by Heather Cahoon
Henry Holt, New York, NY
(2001; 28 pp.)
Grades K–2

If you could ask 10 friends to tea, who would they be? This book provides 10 answers in different number combinations that add up to 10. The grand finale has all 100 friends illustrated. Great story to generate equations and "see" a quantity of 100.

words + math + seasons = Mathematickles!
by Betsy Franco;
illustrated by Steven Salerno
Simon & Schuster, New York, NY
(2003; 32 pp.)
Grades K–4

A collection of poems written in the form of mathematical symbols, charts, graphs, and equations grouped according to seasonal themes. Inspiring for children to create their own equations with words and algebraic symbols.

Internet Sites

Note: While we do our best to provide long-lived addresses in this section, websites can be mercurial! Comparable alternative sites can generally be found with your Web browser.

The Algebra Project
www.algebra.org

Founded by civil rights activist and math educator Robert P. Moses in the 1980s, the Algebra Project is a national mathematics literacy effort aimed at helping low-income students and students of color. The project has developed curricular materials, trained teachers and trainers of teachers, and provided ongoing professional development support and community involvement activities to schools seeking to achieve a systemic change in mathematics education, particularly for African American and Latino/a students.

Early Algebra, Early Arithmetic
www.earlyalgebra.terc.edu

Offers approaches to help young learners examine relationships of numbers and quantities through written notation, tables, and diagrams.

Family Education Network
www.funbrain.com

Offers games for K–8 students as well as resources for teachers and parents. These two games are particularly useful.

Guess the Number
www.funbrain.com/guess/index.html

Calculate the missing number in an equation

Line Jumper Game
www.funbrain.com/linejump/index.html

Locate the answer to computation problems on a number line.

Internet Links for Algebra

www.purplemath.com/internet.htm

The National Center for Improving Student Learning and Achievement in Mathematics and Science at the Wisconsin Center for Education Research, University of Wisconsin-Madison

www.wcer.wisc.edu/ncisla

This center is working with teachers and schools to study and develop ways to advance K–12 students' learning of mathematics and science. Their work is yielding new visions for student achievement and professional development programs that strengthen teachers' content knowledge and in-class practices. The website contains information on education research, publications, and teacher resources.

National Council of Teachers of Mathematics (NCTM)

www.nctm.org

NCTM is a professional organization for teachers of mathematics in grades K–12. The site has resources, lessons, and activities for teachers; information on conferences and other events; descriptions of their many publications; and information on professional development.